S0-BOE-645

Successful Recareering

When Changing *Jobs* Just Isn't Enough

By
Joyce A. Schwarz

CAREER PRESS
180 Fifth Avenue
P.O. Box 34
Hawthorne, NJ 07507
1-800-CAREER-1
201-427-0229 (outside U.S.)
FAX: 201-427-2037

Copyright © 1993 by Joyce A. Schwarz

All rights reserved under the Pan-American and International Copyright Conventions. This book may not be reproduced, in whole or in part, in any form or by any means electronic or mechanical, including photocopying, recording, or by any information storage and retrieval system now known or hereafter invented, without written permission from the publisher, The Career Press.

SUCCESSFUL RECAREERING
WHEN CHANGING JOBS JUST ISN'T ENOUGH
ISBN 1-56414-070-9, $12.95
Cover design by Dean Johnson Design, Inc.
Printed in the U.S.A. by Book-mart Press

To order this title by mail, please include price as noted above, $2.50 handling per order, and $1.00 for each book ordered. Send to: Career Press, Inc., 180 Fifth Ave., P.O. Box 34, Hawthorne, NJ 07507

Or call toll-free 1-800-CAREER-1 (Canada: 201-427-0229) to order using VISA or MasterCard, or for further information on books from Career Press.

Library of Congress Cataloging-in-Publication Data

Schwarz, Joyce A., 1946-
Successful recareering : when changing jobs just isn't enough / by Joyce A. Schwarz.
    p. cm.
  Includes index.
  ISBN 1-56414-070-9 : $12.95
  1. Career changes--United States. I. Title.
HF5384.S38 1993
650. 14--dc20   93-22390
                                                                  CIP

 Dedication

---

To the people who hired us.
To the people who fired us.
And to all of us who dare to
Successfully recareer again and again.

Acknowledgments

To quote William Saroyan, "The foolishness of my writing in comparison with what I wanted to write infuriated me for years. Greatness, Greatness, Greatness is what I wanted and insisted upon...I was long years discovering the secret that it does not matter at all where one begins, and that is not necessary for anything one writes to be instantly great, the most important thing is to resign oneself to the truth that one is only a person and to work..."

As a little girl growing up in a housing project in Ohio, books and magazines were my windows to another world. My first real job in junior high school was selling magazines door to door. Five years later I would work at *Ladies Home Journal* and then edit *American Girl* magazine and go on to a career in advertising and marketing. But even though I helped get dozens of books published and promoted, I was still in awe of book authors.

So now that I am one, let me express my thanks to the following people: to Michael Replogle, who helped me name and develop the first Star*Course classes and so much more—especially during the gestation of this book. To Louise Levison and her buddy Leonard for believing in me even when my faith waivered. To my parents who invested in Joyce Schwarz stock. To my Aunt Hilda, cousin Linda, and Mark Safan and Jerome Zamarin for their patience.

To Luis Loarca for introducing me to the new 486 computer. To Joanie at Medicus for her generosity. To Jeffrey Crausman for listening and guiding me forward. To my earlier career guides Ranny Riley and Judith Claire. To my clients who have successfully recareered and continue to inspire me—including Dr. Linda Seger, Lena Moszkowski, Karen Rubin, Jeffrey Armstrong and Candy Lightner. To my ex-husband, Glenn Schwarz, who saw me through the beginnings of some of the most critical career and life changes.

And to the thousands of other clients, students, audience members and friends who applauded when I spoke, and saw me as the catalyst who helped them to follow their dreams. And finally, thanks to Betsy Sheldon, my editor, for grasping my ideas and my style and honing this into a highly readable book. And to Ron Fry, who believed in me enough to publish *Successful Recareering*.

C Contents

 Introduction

If you are thumbing through this book wondering if it will solve your career problems, be assured that more than 2,000 people have successfully used my system to discover and realize their dream careers. People who've lost their jobs to reorganizations and downsizings. Individuals tired of being overworked, underpaid and unappreciated. The chronically unemployed, and others who still don't know what they want to be when they grow up—at age 30, 40 or even 70.

Whether you dream of playing professional basketball, wonder if you could go back to school and become a doctor, yearn to write and produce your own film, or want to start your own business—this book can be your roadmap to success.

As a career packager and personal marketing expert, I have had the rare opportunity and good fortune to have had people from all walks of life sit across from me in my office. From A to Z, these clients have represented more than 200 professions, including corporate executives, entrepreneurs, Olympic athletes, homemakers, Hollywood film celebrities and television personalities, and even former senatorial and gubernatorial candidates.

Changing careers proved to be a challenge for all of them. But using the techniques I share with you in this book, they have not only succeeded but triumphed in the process. They discovered a new sense of self-fulfillment along the way. You can, too. This book will help you:

- Identify what it is you really want to do—even if you only know what you *don't* want to do right now.

- Discover how *not* to get stuck in the past, by confronting work stereotypes you may have picked up from your family.

- "Try on" your new career for size before committing to your choice.

- Find out which careers are the best bets for the '90s and the new millenium.

- Build a bridge from your current job (or unemployment) to your dream career.

- Future-proof your new career and employment path for the '90s and beyond.

- Determine whether a move—to another location or another country—would be good for you and your career.

- Select role models to inspire you.

- Build your own personal board of advisers from top experts.

Worksheets and skill-building homework exercises in each chapter will help guide you toward your new goals. A supportive, straightforward approach takes all of the mystery out of the transition maze.

Finally, you will learn how to develop the tools that successful athletes, executives and celebrities have used in the past to make dramatic career and lifestyle shifts. An invaluable 18-month career transition plan will show you how to package yourself for success. You can face the new millennium with optimism and personal power.

Why this book?

As we enter the new century, I believe that the American approach to work, our professional goals, the very concept of "career" and our definition of success is being reshaped and redesigned.

President Clinton said in his February 1993 economic address to Congress, "The world is changing so fast that we must have aggressive, targeted attempts to create the high-wage jobs of the future: That's what our competitors are doing."

But perhaps even more importantly to you, the readers of this book, Clinton has also told Americans—prepare to change careers *seven* times during your lives.

That's *careers*—not jobs.

And just as corporations are "reengineering," today, the individual must "recareer"—go through a process of repackaging his or her talents and interests to create and custom-design a fulfilling life and workstyle.

The facts and figures alone are undeniably an impetus for change in the way we work, the way we hire employees, the way we train and the way we fire people. Between 1975 and 1990, the 500 largest U.S. industrial companies failed to add any American jobs according to findings from *The Los Angeles Times*. In 1970, the U.S. ranked first among nations in gross domestic product per capita. Now it has fallen to ninth.

The Indianapolis-based think tank, the Hudson Institute, projects a loss of 2.2 million manufacturing jobs this decade in its study "Workplace 2000." This cutback would mean that for the first time in our modern economy, manufacturing will rank below finance, real estate and insurance as a source of employment.

"We are living through a transformation that will rearrange the politics and economics of the coming century," according to Labor Secretary Robert B. Reich in his much talked-about public policy book, *The Work of Nations*.

And these changes are occurring whether we want them to or not. It used to be that our major fear was speaking in public—it has fast been replaced by the fear of losing our jobs, according to *USA Today*. And number one among life's personal problems is employment (or unemployment) and financial stress according to a St. Paul Fire and Marine Insurance Co. study (December 1992). It found that the problem is so serious that concern about these issues often causes individuals to plummet into deeper troubles.

There's no doubt that there are fewer job opportunities now than at the beginning of the 1980s. The country's largest 500 manufacturers slashed nearly 4 million jobs since 1982. But when *U.S. News & World Report* (June 1993) focuses on a "White Collar Wasteland" and proclaims that a hostile economy has cut short careers for "many of America's best and brightest," it's terrorizing to many who realize that there just may be no relief in sight. In 1993 for the first time ever, white-collar workers have surpassed blue-collar workers in the nation's unemployment lines.

According to our government, the recession officially ended more than two years ago. But white-collar unemployment has kept on climbing from 2.8 million in March 1991 to 3.4 million in late 1992. And as this book goes to press, it has ebbed at 3. 1 million.

U.S. Labor Department statistics show that even last May, when 209,000 new jobs were created, an additional

12

15,000 managers lost their jobs. Statistics indicate that the white-collar jobs are being generated at only half the pace of past recoveries because many industries that were our stalwarts in the past—such as real estate, banking and aerospace—have been hit by financial crises of their own.

Yes, the blue-collar unemployment rate is 9.1 percent (twice that for white-collar workers) but today's work force, from the ivory tower to the mail room, is about 60 percent white-collar.

What does it all mean? Certainly we have entered a *new economy.* And if you look around you, you'll observe people whose lives have changed apparently forever. The woman who sold me my new blue suit (half off!) sparkles when I recognize her artistic eye—she's a graphic artist working two jobs to make ends meet. My insurance agent sighs as she worries aloud that she may never ever again be able to afford to buy a new car. Colleagues who once flashed Platinum American Express cards now meet at fast-food restaurants and jokingly reminisce about the "gourmet '80s."

When Columbia University professor Katherine Newman explores the crisis in her book, *Declining Fortunes,* and says, "If credentials, skills and education can't protect you, then there is no recipe for security in the American job market," it's more than disquieting, it's downright depressing.

And as Harvard economist James Medoff proclaims that only 15 percent of workers displaced in the last recession expect to return to their former jobs, compared with the average of 44 percent in our previous recessions, you start to wonder what the future holds.

When Medoff says in one interview, "People who were primary breadwinners are getting creamed" and in another, "Today, people who lose their jobs are history," you might begin to believe that the best you can do is tread in place.

But I know better. As many of the top experts do, I firmly believe in innovation and technology as the two factors that will redefine the new economy. And I've seen it happening first-hand during the past two years that I've been deeply involved in advising the new breed of entrepreneurs and corporate executives—many of whom are blazing laser and digital trails toward the electronic highways of tomorrow. I've shaken hands and chatted optimistically with the new media leaders like John Sculley of Apple and Silicon Valley's Trip Hawkins as he launched his new 3DO company into play in what he believes will be a $3 trillion telecommunications revolution. It's been exhilarating being on the cutting edge.

And I've worked via modem and fax with a new breed of start-up companies and venture capitalists willing to relocate, revamp and retool if necessary. At professional confabs like Digital World and the National Cable Television Association convention, I've worked side by side with the new *wunderkinds* whose indomitable faith in themselves and the American capitalistic system has inspired them to create a new paradigm for what work is and how it's done. Many have made personal career changes. Scores of other advisers join John Sculley in calling on corporations and the government to institute continuing education, training and retraining programs.

It's my belief that corporate America, as well as our government, has a moral responsibility to retrain America's work force for the future. You can't just upturn an economy and let the workers fall like sand in the winds of change.

But you as individuals have an equal obligation to get your own training to not just keep on track, but to *outpace* change. To lead, not just to follow. Let me reassure you that you, too, can dare to dream again—you can even dare to go for your dream career. Yes, even now.

I'm proud to say that several times every day, my clients, former clients and audience members call me with their successful recareering stories. One went from dietitian to newspaper reporter in less than a month. Another relocated from Washington, D.C., to the greener pastures of North Carolina and found an abundance of film producing opportunities. In the past two weeks, several clients have sold their first books. More than 18 of my clients have successfully made their own major motion pictures—and gotten them into theaters and home video stores. Dozens and dozens of corporate executives who "took the package" have found a better life after "Big Daddy," as they've followed a new career.

It thrills me to have served as a catalyst for these and others who dare to change not just their jobs but their lives. I'm confident that if you follow the career realization process described in this book, it will serve as your catalyst so you, too, can begin to savor success. For some people, the transition takes only weeks. Many others find the 18-month cycle a more reasonable pace. Just remember to build a bridge to your future—because *successful recareering* is a lifelong process.

You'll find new techniques and new methods for researching career options, for sorting out your choices and for reaching prospective employers, partners and business opportunities. The career tools and techniques of yesteryear—massive resume campaigns, informational interviews and want-ad searches are just not enough in this economy. The average job ad in a major metro daily can get more than 500 resumes.

Just another job is not the answer. You need help, guidance and a specific plan of action to discover and create your new career, whether it be your first, your second or your seventh.

So before you sign on the bottom line of the contract for the "Super Duper VIP Rug Cleaners To Go" franchise, or buy the next batch of stamps for 500 more resume letters or grumble one more time about how your boss doesn't appreciate you, start reading and *doing*. And maybe this time you won't just change jobs—you'll change your life!

Go ahead, reach for the stars. After all, the year 2000 is right around the corner.

Why just another job is not enough!

"The need for change bulldozed a road down the center of my mind."

—Maya Angelou
I Know Why the Caged Bird Sings

Any baseball player will tell you that you can't steal second base and keep one foot on first. But many of my clients want to do just that—to slide comfortably from a bad job or no job to a new job that solves all their problems. They want a no-risk home run.

After some soul-searching, however, they discover that they need more than just a change of jobs; they need a change of *career*. And most of the time they yearn to change the very fabric of their lives for the better, too—to weave a dream-come-true.

If you bought this book, this is probably true for you. Even if you've achieved at least some of your dreams— financial success, status in the community, professional rec- ognition—you may now seek a new career. Yet fear, finances or family pressure may be stopping you.

Helen Keller reminds us that, "Life is either a daring adventure or nothing. To keep our faces toward change and behave like free spirits in the presence of fate is strength undefeatable." Noble words, but rough to follow when the going gets tough.

I encourage you to read on. And discover how you can *recareer*—get yourself on a career path that reflects your personality, your personal values, your skills and your lifestyle objectives. During the past few decades, most Americans have followed a one-career philosophy, and the path to multiple careers has been navigated by either the foolhardy, the brave, the mavericks or the pioneers.

Yet, according to my client, anthropologist and author Leanna Wolf, some people have had the urge or necessity to change their occupations ever since the concept of a "profession" evolved more than 5,000 years ago—when society stratified into craftspeople, spinners, farmers, textile workers, weavers and shepherds. Even then people wondered if the grass was greener beyond the next hill.

In this chapter, I'll share several case histories with you. Here's the first one:

This young man began his working life as a bricklayer. Then, after working as a coffin polisher (really), he became a model. He studied acting but then decided to join the Navy. When he got out he found work as a milkman.

Now, what if I told you this man was probably a hero of yours? What if I told you he was a major Hollywood movie star? What if you learned that he has been surrounded by more beautiful women than most men could imagine even seeing in a lifetime? What if I revealed he had played James Bond? Yes, Sean Connery really *was* a bricklayer, coffin polisher, model, officer in the British Royal Navy, milkman and movie star!

In working with people of all backgrounds and professions, I've found a way to ensure that your next career is not just another job. The guiding philosophy of recareering is to have it your way this time. Not just to get a better salary, not just to find something new to do, but also:

- Design a career, custom-tailored to you.
- Create a lifestyle, not just a career.
- Achieve personal fulfillment and make a contribution.

In the past, maybe you "did the right thing," or played it safe, or made a decision and lived with it, or tried but gave up, or were forced to quit before you made it.

Now it's time to have it your way! All of the fast-food chains including McDonalds, Burger King, and Jack in the Box, will make it *their* way, if you don't tell them you want it *your* way. Choosing a career is certainly a more vital choice than whether you want onion or mayo on your fat-free turkey burger. But *you* must make the decision, and how do you do that?

In my counseling and in my life, I've found that the first career comes from decisions made in your head. The *dream* career, however, is prompted by a decision that comes from your gut.

While I was writing this book, I interviewed many VIPs and celebrities, including Robert Townsend, the talented star and director of "Hollywood Shuffle." Townsend used his credit cards to make his own movie. No big bankroll—just plastic and promises to pay actors and crew later. Against the odds, Townsend's movie was picked up by a major Hollywood studio and shown in theaters across the country. But the film would not have happened if Townsend hadn't believed in himself. That's why I wasn't surprised when he told me, "Tell them that the only disgrace in life is not believing in your gut."

"But," you say, "it's not that easy—there's a recession. It's tough out there." Or maybe you're thinking you're too old or you can't teach an old dog new tricks. Or maybe you even changed careers once or twice before. Or you tried starting your own business and it failed. Or you went back to school and it still didn't seem to make a difference. Or...

Stop!

This time it can be different, even if you were just fired today, like John was when he called me. John remembers:

> *"There I was at McDonalds, nursing my third cup of coffee and stabbing my now cold apple pie—pretending it was the guy who canned me that afternoon after three years as an x-ray technician at the City Hospital. I picked up the* LA *Reader (weekly newspaper) and saw Joyce's ad "Make Your Next Career Your Dream Career." I called her from the men's room at McDonalds. She must have thought I had a screw loose. The toilets were flushing around me and there I was, trying to set up a meeting with her immediately. We finally met the next day—Saturday morning. Well, you may not believe this, but by Monday, I was living my dream. I was a TV cameraman—working on a magazine interview show.*

Is John's story extraordinary? You may think so, but I've seen clients and students change their lives in days. *Really.* John followed the 24-hour immersion (described later in Chapter 7) and was living his dream much faster than he ever thought possible.

He still had other challenges to face. But John knew what he wanted to do. He just didn't think it was possible without a lot of training and special schooling. He had explored the work of a cameraman once before and was told by his vocational college career counselors that he had to take a lot of aptitude tests first. Then, his scores showed he was "analytical" and more appropriate for the school's x-ray

19

technician program. Now, there's nothing wrong with apti- tude tests, but many times I find that my recareering can- didates don't need tests—they need to *do the dream.*

With just a few hours of counseling, John emerged with a clear goal and some special transition techniques. He was able to start making his dream come true. Yes, to really *live* the dream he'd have to follow the entire *career realization program*, but he could get started that Monday.

Still not convinced? Maybe you think that because you've been doing the same thing—nursing, accounting, teaching, selling—all your working life, you'll never be able to make a switch without years of education or training in a new area. You might be surprised to realize that if you have at least five years of any kind of work experience, even part-time jobs or raising a family, you are probably pre- pared to make a transition to dozens of different careers.

A college degree is not the deciding factor this time, and you can design your next career, your dream career, even if you're a high school dropout or a new citizen just learning English.

Some of you may be torn between two or three options for your dream career. When Harris first came to me, he wasn't sure which way to turn. He said he was at that pro- verbial fork in the road.

> *"I told Joyce I had two very good options: one to join an advertising agency, which had always been my dream, and the other to join two pals in starting up a new computer graphics company that would do special effects for film, and also enter the new arena of "multimedia" for computer books and games. Both were great opportunities. One with a steady and ter- rific salary; the other where the sky was the limit."*

Which dream to pursue? Wouldn't we all love to have two options! Follow this book's suggestions and you will probably have that many and more. But first ask yourself the same question I asked Harris:

How did you earn your first money in life? What was your first job? How did you feel about that first job? Harris remembers his first job with fondness:

Harris earned his first money combining his love of art (which was considered "sissy" in the 1950s when he was growing up) with his gift of gab. He was 8 in the summer of 1956 and he and his pals were hanging out in homemade forts in the woods near his house. Harris was reaching into his pocket for more ammo for his BB gun when he found a pencil, one that was red on one side and blue on the other. He drew a spectacular serpent on his left arm. When he sported his new "tattoo" to his friends, they begged to have him draw on their arms, too. Harris charged a nickel for a small drawing, and a dime for a large one. He turned his talent into a thriving business, which earned him enough money for a Davy Crockett outfit with chamois chaps and a coonskin cap.

As Harris talked to me, it became clear from his first money-making experience that there were specific aspects of the work that he loved:

- personal freedom
- being a leader
- setting his own pace

The advertising agency would be a culmination of a dream—one he had in high school when the drafting teacher said he'd never get a job in design because his work was too sloppy. But the computer graphics opportunity would be a career for now and the future. One that he could design himself, one that would offer personal freedom as well as a chance to lead the pack. He has chosen that path.

Almost everyone has a childhood story about work. Here are two more:

Hollywood producer and host Dick Clark (of American Bandstand fame) tells the tale of his first job—shining shoes. He says that all the kids in the neighborhood were out that summer with polish and rags and even fancy shoeshine kits. Clark went back into his house after eyeing the competition and used his crayons to draw up a sign that said, "One shoe shined 3 cents, two shoes shined 5 cents," and he garnered more business than the rest of the kids because of his ingenuity. Is it any wonder that, today, Clark is a mega-mogul whose company has produced 34 series, 50 television specials and 27 made-for-TV movies? He certainly knows how to close a deal.

Karen, one of my clients who now runs her own catering service, got her start making scones and selling them at church bake sales. Her scones were famous county wide. As Karen's plans for her new business formed, she realized what she loved most about her baking activity. She loved watching people taste her scones and having them tell her how good they were. Today, she has another chef make the food for her catering firm, someone else to manage the business, and always handles the sales herself and attends the events so she can keep in touch with her clients.

The *why* of your second career choice is more important than the *what*. For many people in the 1930s and 1940s, getting a good job was the goal. You pounded the pavement, you hit up relatives or friends, and you wangled your way into anything that was out there—and you stayed there. It was a steady job and what you *wanted* wasn't as important as the regular paycheck.

Along the way in your jobs or your careers, you may have been talked down to, pushed aside, passed over or stepped on. These experiences may have thwarted you from your dreams. Just as it's good to look at the best job experiences, it's important to look at the worst ones, too, so that you don't include them in your design for your dream career.

What were your worst experiences on the job? They may have been humiliating. They may have been failures you blame on your own ignorance or arrogance, or because you had a bad boss. Or simply because you didn't yet know yourself.

For example, Sharon, who made jewelry and sold it at flea markets, says:

> *"I invested in a jewelry-making class and an ex-pensive kit. I designed some great stuff—I really had talent, if I must say so myself. But it didn't sell. No one was willing to pay even the price I'd paid for the beads. I finally sold a couple of pieces and then the people brought them back the next week—the fasteners had broken. I just couldn't win—I guess I just wasn't made to have my own business."*

Well, it probably wasn't the business that was bad. Sharon's materials may have been overpriced, and apparently of poor quality. Her sales techniques may not have been effective. After talking to Sharon, it seems that she hated standing out in the sun all alone trying to sell. She loved to create. Maybe a partner would be her ideal addition, to make her dream career come true.

More often than not, I find that it's not the dream that fails, but rather the implementation of the dream that's wrong. When it comes to knowing the right dream career for you, your gut is usually right. But your timing may be off. You might have too many pressures. Maybe not enough emotional support.

Many people believe that just changing their job will change their life. And in truth, changing a job can provide some emotional and financial relief—a change of scenery, a more understanding boss and a raise. If you've been unemployed, just being "back in the saddle" again may be enough—for awhile. But then, you may experience that old nagging feeling—there must be something more.

And there is for many of you. Some of you may be ready to go for your dream career now. Others may want to make plans now and go for it in the future. What guidelines should you use for determining if you're ready *now* or if you should get a J.O.B.? I call it a J.O.B. because you choose this job consciously, for its benefits, especially its opportunity to build a bridge to your dream career. (J.O.B. stands for Just Only a Bridge.) A J.O.B. is something that you do to earn a living, to put the whole-wheat bread and cholesterol-free spread on your table.

You may want to choose a J.O.B. if:

1. You are in a financially unstable part of your life.

2. You are in a life crisis or a personal crisis—heading toward a divorce, in the midst of a custody battle, dealing with an aging parent.

3. You are emotionally burned out.

4. You've recently relocated to a new area.

5. You are just out of school and don't know which way to turn.

A J.O.B. can provide you with a breather, needed health benefits, an opportunity to get necessary skills to move forward, a chance to go back to school and study for your dream career, and maybe even a chance to meet VIPs who will be helpful in setting up your own business, especially if you're new to the area.

A *dream career* evolves when you "package" your skills, your aptitudes and expertise with your personal interests and values to create your own ideal livelihood. Most dream careers are *created*, they don't just happen. And re-member, you're designing a lifestyle this time—not just an-other way to make money.

If you think you're ready for a dream career, but still can't sort out what you want to do, try to remember a time in your life when you did something that made you feel special—paid or unpaid. As a kid, I loved being in school pageants, emceeing events and reading my essays aloud in class. When people applauded, it was music to my ears and my heart. And when a teacher or classmate came up afterward to say that my words had affected them, I glowed. It was fun, it was rewarding and it made me feel special. Today, I an well-paid for my classes and public speaking. But nothing beats the internal reward I get from this work.

In their book, *Winning the Change Game*, my former client Kathy Farrell and her co-author Craig Broude describe the steps necessary to make a change in a company's information system. Not surprisingly, these steps seem to work just as well in making life changes.

When we're moving from an old system to a new system—say, from never using a computer to being fully automated—the beginning steps result in feelings of incompetence and insecurity. Following is a big middle ground where the user feels stressed, frustrated and worn.

You'll probably feel all of these feelings. If you're moving from the comfort zone of a job, you may want to follow the authors' suggestion to list the steps ahead, set specific objectives, create bridges, develop schedules and action plans, and reinforce your progress (with rewards).

In working with my clients and my own careers, I've found that there are seven guidelines to follow in the *career realization process*:

1. Believing in your gut.
2. Suspending disbelief.
3. Identifying your dream.
4. Selecting your lifestyle.
5. Using the right tools to design the right plan.
6. "Test-driving" your career through the 24-hour immersion.
7. Implementing your plan and living your dream.

The next nine chapters will provide you with step-by-step methods for realizing your dream career. These methods have been used by thousands of my clients and students. The 24-hour immersion is a special technique so that you don't get to your "goal" and then realize, like many people, that the dream career may not be right for you after all.

This book will provide you with homework assignments (optional) and worksheets. I refer to the experiences of my clients, myself and well-known celebrities to give you a sense that—yes, successful recareering can be done by all kinds of people in all walks of life.

Along the way, you'll probably have to deal with pressures from *them*—your spouse, your parents, your boss, your colleagues—everyone who knows how to live your life better than you do, or so they say. That's why you'll want to turn to the next chapter and find out why you were right and they were wrong. And what to do about it now and forever.

Homework

1. Make a list of what you'd do if you won $1 million.
2. Name the one thing you must do before you begin to pursue your dream.
3. Determine how you can begin to pursue your dream career even if you're financially stuck or in the midst of a personal crisis.
4. List all of the things that are easy for you to do—your talents, abilities and skills. How do they apply to your dream career?
5. What will your family and friends think about your decision to pursue your dream career?

1. Suspending disbelief

In order to move forward with your dream career, it's important to be able to suspend disbelief. In other words, you don't have to believe you can do the dream career at first, but you do have to suspend your disbelief that you *can't* do it. Here are some exercises that may help.

1. Did you ever see a UFO? Did you believe there was a logical explanation for the mysterious appearance, or were you open to the possibility that it was really a UFO?

_____

_____

_____

_____

_____

_____

_____

_____

2. Has anything "miraculous" ever happened to you? Like winning money just when you needed it most? What were your feelings about this?

_____

_____

_____

_____

_____

_____

_____

3. If you could have been born in the 19th century, what would you have done for a dream career?

_____

_____

_____

_____

_____

_____

_____

_____

4. If you could have been born in the Wild West era, what would you have done as a dream career (cowboy/frontiers-woman/sheriff)?

_____

_____

_____

_____

_____

5. If you could have been born in another time, when would it have been? And what would you have done?

_____

_____

_____

_____

_____

_____

_____

2. Your job satisfaction history

Your first job

1. How well did you like your first job?

_____

_____

_____

2. Did you like your boss? What about the people you worked with?

_____

_____

_____

3. If you could have changed your first job, how would you have changed it?

_____

_____

_____

_____

4. If you could have been your boss, how would you have treated *you* as an employee?

_____

_____

_____

Your best job

1. What was the job you loved the most?

_____

_____

_____

2. List three things you loved about it.

_____

_____

_____

3. How would you like doing that same job today?

_____

_____

_____

4. Why were you happy at your favorite job?

_____

_____

_____

_____

5. How can you take some of the things that made you happy in your favorite job and include them in your dream career?

_____

_____

_____

_____

_____

6. What's the one thing that's important for you to have in your dream job so that you'll enjoy it?

_____

_____

_____

_____

_____

_____

You were right, and they were wrong

"Is there ever any particular spot where one can put one's finger and say, 'It all began that day at such a time and such a place, with such an incident?'"
—Agatha Christie

Odds are, your family had a great deal of influence on the career path you've taken up until now. This may have been good. You may have come from a family where personal fulfillment through work was encouraged. Your interests and skills may have been nourished by your parents through lessons and guidance.

Or your parents' influence on your career direction may *not* have been so positive. Maybe they pushed you into a prestigious profession—like law or medicine—even though your interests ran to the arts. They may have belittled your ambitions and made you believe that you'd never succeed. Perhaps, if you are a woman, they convinced you that nice girls didn't worry about getting ahead and how much money they should make.

Whether you feel your parents and family had a positive or negative effect on your career, you should examine their influence on your choices now—to make sure you are headed in a direction that you believe is good for you.

The effect our families have on our performance in the workplace is just beginning to be explored. When I studied organizational psychology 20 years ago at the University of San Francisco, it was not a part of the program. That stuff was for the "pop psychologists." Home was home and work was work and the twain did not meet.

While there isn't a lot of definitive research on the topic, you'd better believe that your family relationships played a big role in your career decisions—and more.

Look at Norman Lear, for example. The talented writer and TV producer grew up in a family where his parents lived with constant bickering and one-upmanship. Out of that situation, he chose to make a positive statement about a negative view of life in the form of comedy. As a result he wrote, "Divorce American Style," "All in the Family," and "Maude."

In her book *Megatraits*, Dr. Doris Lee McCoy says, "The miracle of birth provides us with a number of givens: intellectual ability, physical stature, predisposition to medical conditions. We are born into a situation with a given set of parents who determine our early lives, they provide us with a set of basic values that comes from their own belief systems. Although, we have the freedom to change those values later, we are nonetheless influenced by our heritage. It is up to us to discover or rediscover the guiding philosophy that gives us direction and inner peace."

Let's consider Susan:

> *"Mom always wanted a job, but dad was adamant that she couldn't work—it would make him look bad even if we needed the money, which we did sometimes desperately. Somehow, Dad's suppression of Mom consciously or unconsciously influenced me to*

have a career. I've worked my whole life at one job or another, but it really didn't matter what I did as long as I was working. I've been a teacher and a principal and now a customer sales representative for a computer company. What I really want to do is to start a nursery school—but somehow, I just can't get it together to start it."

You don't need to be a psychologist to see that Susan may be identifying too closely with her mother's role as caretaker at home. Susan may need some counseling to help her determine what is really *her* dream.

"Family" may be such an overwhelming topic to you, you don't even want to get close to it. Yet, I find that if you don't explore your reasons for selecting past careers and jobs and the influence your family had upon you, you are never quite free enough to choose your own dream career.

A not-so-funny thing happened to my client John on the way to his dream career as a TV cameraman: His fiancee threatened to leave him unless he went back to his job at the hospital, his dad demanded back the money he paid for John's x-ray technician schooling, and his brothers told him he was crazy to try something new. John is not alone, many families play the same games.

If you're unemployed, in transition, or even considering reentering the job marketplace, you know *they're* standing there breathing heavy down your back and pressuring you to play it safe. In fact, you may be facing even more pressure from your family, who may be embarrassed, ashamed or fearful about your job loss.

Take a moment to think which way your family has hurt or helped you in your career/job choices. In selecting your previous jobs were you trying to rebel? Or keep peace?

Time after time, my clients who gave up their early dreams say to me, "I remember the day I announced to my parents that I wanted to be (fill in the blank)." And then they describe a scenario that goes something like this:

Mom: *"When are you going to get a real job and settle down?"*

Son: *"Mom, you don't understand, I want to do something special."*

Dad: *"Something special isn't going to put food on the table. Listen to your mother!"*

Many people just got worn down by their family's nagging. And they gave in. Here's what I hear from my clients who didn't pursue their dreams:

"My dad was a lawyer and so was my grandpa. I couldn't get out of it."

"Mom had dreamed her whole life I'd be a doctor."

"I came back from Vietnam and my brother-in-law was the only one who offered me a job."

"I majored in history, so my parents assumed I'd teach."

"In my day, you were either a mom, a teacher or a nurse—maybe a stewardess if you were really adventurous."

"Somebody had to run the family store."

Or maybe you were one of those late bloomers, who really didn't have a clue as to what you wanted to do for a living when you got out of high school or college. *They* said it was time to support yourself, so you got a job. Economics itself is usually not the only reason for giving up the dream.

Class distinction or economic status does *not* seem to affect family influence on career direction. Families from all walks of life put pressure on their children—whether it's affluent families directing their children to pursue Ivy League schools and careers in law or medicine, or working-class parents pressuring their kids to do better than they did.

Perhaps career dreams should come with this:

> **WARNING: *The advice of family and friends may be hazardous to your happiness.***

There is an old Navajo saying: "A man can't get rich if he takes proper care of his family," and there is a certain amount of truth in this. When it comes to your dream career, though, you must take proper care of yourself first.

All too often my clients say that it is family obligations that stop them from moving forward. "If I weren't married," and "If I didn't have kids" are the two laments I hear most frequently. Women may feel it is their duty to stay home with the kids, and feel guilty about pursuing their own interests. Parents worry that their children will suffer from the latchkey syndrome—feel neglected or get into trouble. And both mother and father may avoid making a career change for fear of risking the financial security of the family.

These concerns are valid, but not insurmountable. There are creative solutions. Seeking out businesses that offer on-site day care, starting a business in the home or working part-time are all options to explore. The point is, you may need to compromise because of the needs of your family—but you shouldn't give up your career goals. In fact, study after study indicates that children whose parents are fulfilled career-wise tend to be emotionally healthy, well-adjusted and self-confident.

In the dream career, *you* come first

It's surprising that people who control what they wear, what they eat and how they think, still let their family influence how they spend the rest of their lives.

The happy ending of "It's a Wonderful Life," evokes tears as Jimmy Stewart's character realizes how rich he became in following the career path that others—his family and his town—wanted him to take. But let's just imagine how much *richer* he might have felt had he asked his guardian angel what things would have been like if he had lived the exciting life that he'd always dreamed of—rather than wishing he was never born.

What steps can you take, other than years of therapy, to get past the influence your family may have over your career directions and your potential for success?

1. Talk to your parents. Sometimes it's best to confront your parents directly. Some clients choose to write a letter to their parents telling them how they feel about their dream careers. Parents may not have realized the hurtful effect they may have on their children and, once aware, may be more supportive.

2. Or...*don't* talk to your parents! Keep your phone calls focused on the weather, and leave your family out of your discussions of plans and activities related to your dream career. If you're sure you'll get criticism, skepticism and discouragement, there's no point in subjecting yourself to it.

3. Examine your past. Is there something in your family background that is holding you back? Identify the comments or actions your parents took in regard to your future. Were they discouraging? Did they force you into a direction you didn't want to go in? What can you do to change that?

37

4. Examine your parents' past. Have your mother or father expressed deep regrets about their own career choices? Did one of them have a bad attitude about his or her own job? See if you can identify those attitudes or incidents that may have affected you.

5. Get professional help. If you can't boot the family skeletons out of your closet, work on them in private therapy.

6. Create a family of choice. As an adult, you can choose to surround yourself with friends, mentors and people who believe in you. These people, your family of *choice,* may be much more important than your parents in helping you achieve your goals.

What's fascinating is to go back and to see if you're still playing your family games. These are the most frequent games I hear my clients talk about. Of course, there are lots of variations.

Follow the leader

If you're male, were you encouraged to follow in your dad or grandfather's path? If you're female, did it matter more what your apple pie tasted like than whether you got an "A" in physics? Gail Sheehy in her book, *Pathfinders*, calls this the "Father's Footstep Disease."

Puppet on a string

Were you ever or are you now a "puppet" that your parents are manipulating to live out their own dreams. Some people's parents are master ventriloquists. In fact, some don't even have to be near you in the workplace to have you simulate their conditioned responses.

Musical chairs

So you were the one elected to be the lawyer and your sister was the nun and your brother was the engineer? Some parents have preconceived notions of where their children should sit and just line up the slots like a game of musical chairs.

Checkers or chess masters

Many parents pit one kid against another. Or one parent becomes the queen and the other the king, and the kids are just pawns. These familial relationships are then played and replayed as the child enters the work force. You may "reinvent" your parent in the form of a boss or supervisor in the workplace. Or maybe in a personal relationship.

It's time to play by *your* rules!

This time, you're in charge. Here are the new games I suggest you begin playing today to let go of some of the family influences that may still be lurking:

1. You're the leader. You make your own choices this time.
2. You pull your own strings. Move step by step forward to your goal.
3. You play both sides of the checkerboard.
4. You keep the king and queen in your own pocket. Your chances of winning the game are much stronger than if you give your power to someone else.

Sometimes the games are fuzzier. Here are some of the most frequently cited problems among my clients, and here are my suggestions on how to use them as *opportunities* in designing your dream career:

Problem: Not enough attention from my family!
Opportunity: Take the lead, be a star. Make sure you build in positive feedback opportunities and even applause in your new career.

Problem: My family knew it all.
Opportunity: Teach others part time, coach or share your talents. Your students will acknowledge you for what *you* know this time.

Problem: My sibling was better at...
Opportunity: Consult as part of your dream career or work in a team-based environment, as opposed to a competitive environment.

Problem: My parents were always arguing.
Opportunity: Become a master negotiator. Try humor or learn to protect your personal boundaries at work.
Problem: They made fun of me.
Opportunity: Share the gift of laughter, do something where the new "they" appreciate you because you are different.

Problem: They didn't care.
Opportunity: Consider taking on a caring partner, surround yourself with a supportive team—both inside and outside of the workplace.

Tina's family never really cared what she did. They were too busy worrying about her brother, who was a juvenile delinquent. Her good grades and her accomplishments went unnoticed. She decided to start her own business later in life and found that it put her out there alone again. She loved the work but found it emotionally unfulfilling. She realized what she needed, and began to seek the support she was denied as a child.

Her boyfriend got involved in the business by attending trade shows with her and recommending her to everyone he knew. She built a supportive team of employees at work, and continued to develop her network of contacts. These were changes that helped her turn her business into her dream career.

Many times, family, especially spouses, can be important in helping you reach your goal. No one can do it alone—and I mean no one. Not even the experts. Not even the people who write the books about it.

Norman Vincent Peale *almost* didn't write *The Power of Positive Thinking*. He was told that his approach was all wrong. It was his wife, Ruth, who supported him and encouraged him to continue. The book has sold more than 15 million copies since 1952.

George Burns once said, "Happiness is having a large, loving close knit family in another city." You may find that to really make your next career your dream career, you may have to disconnect from your family for at least a while. Am I saying you have to do a "Gauguin" and go to Tahiti? No, but you may choose to relocate. If you're living at home, you may choose to live with friends. You may even take a breather from socializing with certain relatives every week while you're making the transition.

Do not underestimate the power of your family, but do not *overestimate* it either. Be prepared by establishing a strong support system that will include people you select.

Homework

1. Make a list of all the negative things your family said to you. Then substitute the good things you wanted them to say. For example, replace "Dave's not a good enough student to study anything as difficult as law," to "Dave is capable of doing anything he puts his mind to."

2. Make a list of the good things you have learned from your family. We all learn something even from the worst family situations—even if it's just not to repeat that cycle of behavior.

3. You may have started to form a family of choice already. Make a list of all those individuals who would support you emotionally in your dream career.

4. Is there a talent you inherited or a skill you learned from your parents that you yearn to build into a business? Many of my female clients learned about business from hearing their dads talk about their businesses at the dinner tables. Take the best and use it!

3. Your family's work history

1. What's the first comment about work you remember someone in your family making?

_____
_____
_____

2. What did/do your parents do?

_____
_____
_____

3. What did your grandparents do?

_____
_____
_____

4. Did your mother work ouside of the home when you were growing up? If so, what was your attitude toward her working? What was your father's attitude?

_____
_____
_____
_____

5. How do you feel the economy and workplace have changed since your father's and mother's day?

_____
_____
_____
_____

6. How has the economy and workplace changed since your grandparents' day?

_____

_____

7. Who in your family changed careers? Describe the changes they made.

_____

_____

_____

8. Did anyone in your family (adults) *not* work?

_____

_____

9. What was the attitude in your family toward someone who was not working?

_____

_____

10. Was work equated with money?

_____

11. Was work equated with power?

_____

12. Did anyone in your family have a dream career? If so, what was it?

_____

_____

13. Did anyone want a dream career who was not able to have one? If so, why?

_____

_____

_____

_____

4. How your family influenced you

1. What did your family say to encourage your career dreams?

_____

_____

_____

_____

2. What did your family *do* to encourage you (pats on the back, rewards)?

_____

_____

_____

_____

3. How would you like your family to encourage you today?

_____

_____

_____

_____

4. How can you get that encouragement if you don't get it from your family?

_____

_____

_____

_____

5. When did your family discourage you? What did they say?

_____

_____

_____

_____

6. When and how did your family let you down (not showing up at an event, etc.)?

_____

_____

7. Did your siblings ever make fun of what you were doing?

_____

_____

8. Did you ever encourage your parents or siblings on their projects?

_____

_____

9. Do you feel you've encouraged people in your family more/less that they've encouraged you?

_____

_____

10. What complaints do you still have about your family?

_____   _____

_____   _____

_____   _____

_____   _____

11. What were your siblings better at than you were?

_____

_____

12. What were you better at than your siblings?

_____

_____

5. Value clarification

In settting up your dream career path, you may want to be sure that your dreams are realized this time—not your family's. Use this worksheet to clarify *your* values rather than your family's desires.

1. My family wants me to _____

_____

I want to _____

_____

2. Regarding work, my family believes _____

_____

I believe _____

_____

3. In terms of importance, my work is _____percent of my life.
My family felt work was_____ percent.

4. My family worked for the following reasons:

_____   _____

_____   _____

5. I work because:

_____

_____

6. Other than working, I make my dreams come true by:

_____

_____

_____

_____

# Adapting
the future
workplace

> "One machine can do the work of fifty ordinary
> men. No machine can do the work of one extraordi-
> nary man."
>
> Elbert Hubbard
> *The Roycroft Dictionary and Book of Epigrams*

Your father may have sold his soul to the company store, or the family business. But for you and your kids, that option may not exist; the store has probably been sold and the family company may be on the brink of bankruptcy.

"It's rough out there" says Harvey Mackay, author of the self-protection guide *Sharkproof*. He believes, "The worried people are the ones who've got the jobs."

Certainly, the figures are not comforting. In January 1993, 106,617 jobs were cut by 34 companies, according to the Bloomberg Business News. And William Morin, chairman of outplacement firm Drake Beam Morin, estimates that roughly a quarter of the U.S. work force is still imperiled by downsizing.

Suddenly, technology and economic forces are changing our job opportunities, and our workstyles as well. Corporate downsizings, reorganizations, efficiency programs, early retirement plans: They're all new terms for what may be the excuse for your pink slip—and impetus for your job or career change. And, as the economy recovers, previously laid-off employees are discovering that their jobs may *not* be reinstated. In fact, many particular functions are becoming obsolete, forcing many to consider not just a new employer, but a new career.

The good news is that there is no disgrace today in changing jobs or careers. The phrase "job hopper" will not be automatically stamped on your new resume. In fact, there is a new respectability for changing careers in today's marketplace. And a new necessity, also.

Experts say that the average job today lasts three to four years. If you're 40 today, that means you could squeeze in an astounding seven more jobs before the traditional retirement age!

Your best bet against the fickleness of today's job economy may indeed be to pursue your dream career or *careers*, based on your personality, your own goals, your own lifestyle choices and your personal values.

Sure, it may seem risky to begin a new career now, but the reward may be greater, too—especially personally and emotionally. One of the most important trends in our society today is a new determination to control our own destinies. James Taylor, CEO of the well-respected research firm Yankelovich Partners, reports that only 12 percent of the people he surveyed trust public statements made by corporations, but an unprecedented 7 out of 10 people agree with the statement, "I'm the one in charge of my life."

That certainly was not the employee slogan of your parents' day. The old-style career path of working your way up the corporate ladder is gone.

What does this mean to you? Well, it's like learning how to play football one day and then having them change the rules at half-time to field hockey—you may have the wrong equipment, you may not know what to do next, and you may have coaches and mentors who are also out of date.

Change means opportunity in new areas

In the future, certain careers may be deleted in the same amount of time it takes to press that key on your computer. After all, in our lifetimes we have already seen the death of such jobs as computer punch card operator, elevator operator, home television repair and more.

And the demand for other jobs, many that were non-existent 20 years ago, is increasing. According to the U.S. Bureau of Labor Statistics, here are a few of the fastest-growing jobs in America for the next decade:

Paralegal personnel
Medical assistant
Physical therapist
Physical therapist assistant
Data processing equip-
    ment repairer

Podiatrist
Computer system analyst
Medical records technician
Employment interviewer
Home health aide

10 trends revolutionizing the workplace of the future

1. The rise of service industries. As more women enter the work force, and all workers struggle with less free time and greater demands, more than 70 percent of all businesses will be service-oriented. Personalized shopping, home-delivered gourmet meals and dating services are some of the burgeoning businesses, while childcare, home cleaning and home health care are traditional service businesses that will continue to see growth.

2. New technology. The merging of entertainment, consumer electronics, telephone companies, cable and the computer worlds will create a vast new world of career opportunities in telecommunications.

During the writing of this book, I was fortunate to meet former Apple Computer CEO John Sculley at the National Association of Broadcasters Conference. It was Sculley who told President Clinton the "continuing reorganization of work itself" is part of a social transformation as massive and as wrenching as the industrial revolution.

Sculley feels it's impossible to determine the impact of new technology and the national information infrastructure on our lives. He estimates that by the year 2000, the three industries of telecommunications (at about $1.2 trillion) and the media (at about $1.3 trillion) and the combined industries of consumer electronics and computers (at $1 trillion) will add up to an amazing $3.5 trillion. (Today's gross national product for our country is only $6 trillion total.)

3. Telecommuting. Some experts predict that as many as 60 percent of the working population will work, at least part of the time, from their home by the year 2000. Videophones, modems and fax machines will make it easier than ever to work from anywhere in the world.

4. The emergence of the minority as the majority. Racial and ethnic diversity will be the norm—in both the workplace and the marketplace, as Generation X (the generation of Americans born between 1965 and 1985) emerges into adulthood. The largest segments will be whites, African-Americans, Hispanic-Americans and Asian-Americans. Such diversification will mean more balanced representation and treatment of "minorities," as employees as well as consumers. So if you're staffing an office, forming a start-up company or selling a product or service, a multi-cultural approach is a necessity.

51

5. Creation of the *new entrepreneur*. Millions of people will develop their own companies using imagination and innovation as their guides. In the '80s, we saw the creation of new businesses—personal training, personal nutrition, dog-sitting services and home computer consulting. In the '90s, we'll see pick-up dinner services, lifestyle consultants and home entertainment planners.

6. The greening of the workplace. Just as the need for equal opportunity specialists grew in the '70s, the demand for environmental impact consultants will increase in the workplace as individuals and businesses alike recognize the need to protect and preserve our natural resources.

7. The elimination of "ageism." As the population continues to age, discrimination will diminish. It may be an advantage to be older in order to serve an older market in the year 2000 and beyond.

8. Revolutions in education and training. New technology and privatization of portions of the educational system will be the impetus for a new emphasis on learning. Corporations like Disney are already exploring new educational opportunities and co-ventures, including in-school television systems. Director George Lucas is deeply involved in interactive teaching programs. Cable television projects and the information highway will bring quality in-home learning to the masses.

9. A change in retail selling. Malls continue to crop up, but the way we shop, what we buy and where we buy is changing rapidly with the invasion of new technology in the home and in public spaces. Computer shopping and home shopping via the TV will have an impact on advertising, marketing and direct-mail industries.

10. The global neighborhood. Business and personal relationships will change dramatically as we begin to interact with people from lands not so foreign anymore because of the internationalism of our economy. New computer programs allowing instantaneous translation will enable us to communicate with Milan as easily as with Miami.

What do other experts predict?

If you look at a couple of books on the future, you may be inspired to develop your dream career based on some of these forecasted trends. For example in *Megatrends 2000, Ten New Directions for the '90s,* John Naisbitt and Patricia Aburdene list these following trends. Following each trend I've included some examples that may inspire you to take this knowledge and apply it to your own career aspirations:

1. Renaissance in the arts. David and Jane are buying an inn in Maine and will operate a summer stock theater out of its barn. In addition to the restaurant and hotel income, the profits they make from the theater will allow them to close the inn during the cold winters.

2. The emergence of free market socialism. Financial planner Kurt returned from an extended vacation in Hungary and is now helping Hungarian entrepreneurs set up businesses with American partners.

3. Global lifestyles and cultural nationalism. Frank is taking advantage of the fact that 80 percent of all information now stored in computers is in English. He is now in Japan teaching English to Japanese executives and using his videotape knowledge to tape their efforts, giving him a "techno-edge" on his competitors.

Real estate entrepreneur Jane Coe set up an office in Madrid and one in Milan and communicates via modem from her home in Beverly Hills. She lives in Madrid in the summer, Milan in the spring, and she's looking for a fall office in Australia, which will give her two springs—her favorite season.

4. Privatization of the welfare state. Carol has gotten more than 40,000 people off welfare through her nonprofit organization that provides education and job training.

But what about *you*?

So with all of this change how do you decide what to do? My background tells me that job selection becomes much more personalized. You don't just find a new career, you *package* your career for the '90s and beyond. You realize that you may have more than seven careers and you build bridges along the way to your future so that you are not left adrift in the ocean of change.

How to be prepared for the year 2000

- Become an entrepreneur. (Some experts believe 70 percent of all jobs may be entrepreneurial by the year 2000).
- Find a company where you can be an *intrapreneur* (you run your department and are rewarded for new ideas, products and services).
- Search for a company that is liberal with its employee stock options, where you can cash into the future by betting on it. (As many as 2,000 or more employees may have become millionaires by betting on Bill Gates' Microsoft success by taking stock options.)
- Choose a transition career or careers so you can learn skills leading to your dream career.

- Have a combo-career—part transition career or part J.O.B. and part dream career.
- Relocate and start your dream career or recreate some variation of your old J.O.B.

Determining whether this is the time in your life to pursue your dream career is something you'll want to explore with qualified counselors, accountants, supportive people in your "family of choice" and your personal board of advisers. And then *you* still have to make the final decision—whether you want to open a restaurant, go into teaching or build a bed-and-breakfast resort in the mountains.

Do you have to be a techno-whiz, or propeller-head to thrive in the new future economy? No. In fact the U.S. Department of Labor forecasts that the country will need twice as many school teachers, three times as many nurses and five times as many retail clerks and computer analysts. Some experts feel that the computer engineer of today will become like the railroad engineers of the 20th century—just people doing their jobs to keep things "rolling along."

What is certain, is that the way we work, the way we sell, the way we educate our kids, and the way we communicate, will change dramatically in our lifetimes.

Soon computer bulletin boards, computer networks, desktop video conference and new pocket-size videophones will make it easy to communicate with anyone, anywhere in the world.

What can you do personally?

To make sure that you're ready for the future, I recommend to my clients to follow these six guidelines:

1. Find your special talent. As Dr. Doris Lee McCoy says in *MegaTraits*, "If you find or have found your special niche/talent it will set you free to be all you can be. Success will surely follow."

Tanya left her job as an investment banker after a bad auto accident confined her to her home. During that three-month period as an invalid, she began to explore her dream of setting up a record company and selling the tapes of her singing at charity events and conventions, in which she customized company literature and folklore into witty tunes. She may never get rich, but she's recovered from the accident completely. And her financial settlement combined with her savings and her entertainment gigs give her a comfortable income.

Is Tanya an exception? No! I have hundreds of clients who are pursuing their dream careers using their own special talents. Some of them are not as fortunate as Tanya, and their nest eggs have run out or their spouses are supporting them. Other clients work part-time to support themselves and their families, and pursue their talents (stand-up comedy, acting) at night or on weekends. But most of them are very happy and believe that this will work out for them in the long run.

2. Reinvent what you've been doing, or reinvent your method of working. Even something as straightforward as telephone sales has been changed dramatically by the autodialer. Today, everything, from BMWs to artwork to environmentally correct light bulbs, is sold via the phone. Some of my clients work from their home doing telephone sales or selling their own inventions or food products while their kids are still growing up. Others are working at part-time job-sharing programs and pursuing their dream on off days.

3. Invent a new career, a new product or a new service that fits the demand of today's marketplace. Home delivery of office supplies for entrepreneurs could become a service as welcome as milk and egg delivery in the '40s. Emergency computer software advice via 900-phone lines could make a savvy consultant rich.

4. Give *extra* service. No one wants just another computer technician. *Everyone* wants a computer consultant who is available 24 hours a day via beeper and who accepts credit cards and makes house calls. Especially if he or she can troubleshoot and charges reasonable prices.

5. If you don't know where to start—go back to that first job you loved and combine it with your life skills. Add a bit of new technology and you may create some magic. My first job *was* my dream career. Working on a magazine was all I ever wanted to do from the age of 13. An electronic, interactive magazine would be an excellent "technobet" for me for the future. (Interactive television and interactive film may combine to form $10 billion in interactive entertainment revenues in the U.S. by the year 2000.)

6. Cash in on serendipity. If an intriguing opportunity just falls in your lap, you may want to go for it. Don't bet your piggybank on it, but you may want to invest some time pursuing the venture if you don't have any other options that are bright right now. Once again, turn to your board of advisers or your "family of choice" to get their input first—and then let your gut guide you.

Personally, I encourage my clients to think in three arenas when thinking about dream careers for the future:

1. High-tech/high-touch approaches
2. Low-tech solutions
3. High-touch concepts

High-tech/high-touch approaches

- The video phone—adding a sense of intimacy with a high-tech product.

- Computer bulletin boards, especially the ones that allow you to interact to play games, share recipes or swap photos of products for sale. You come up with your own new bulletin board, driven by people's needs, not technology's demands.

- Video greeting cards and personalized computer greetings that feature real faces, names and a chance to custom-tailor the message.

Low-tech solutions

- Audio tape magazines, videotape crafts workshops, cable access TV shows.

- Infomercials for your herbal hair thickener product.

- 800-number referral services of computerized bartering systems.

High-touch solutions

- Selling your family's favorite "shoo fly pie" to the local restaurants for their diners to discover.

- Using your sales skills to develop "Selling for the '90s" seminars.

- Turning your farm into a "farm-and-breakfast" experience for city slickers.

Skills to keep pace with the workplace

How to cash in on the new technology and the future? I recommend that you pursue proficiency in the following skills in order to be ready for the workplace of the next millennium:

1. Computer literacy. At the very least, you need to develop computer *familiarity*. You can learn the basics in a weekend—*really*. It's helpful to be familiar with both IBM compatible and Macintosh.

If you've never used a computer, take a class at your community college, free university or a private school. For less than $100 you'll begin to join the Information Age. In less than four hours you'll be keyboarding along on a word processing program. Proficiency may take months but basic skills can be learned in days. Even for the most serious technophobic, *I cannot stress how important this is*.

2. Access to fax. If you do not own a fax machine, find an office services outlet nearby where you can have ready access to one.

3. Computerized mailing list—and means to update it. If you're starting your own business, be sure to have at least 2,000 names as well as sources for additional contacts. This is the absolute minimum. And you will want to communicate with these people quarterly at the least.

4. Knowledge of Spanish. Or French, Japanese, Chinese, Russian or another language appropriate to the business you're in. As the world community shrinks to a global village, your comfort with a foreign language will become more important.

5. Project-oriented work vs. steady paycheck. Tom Peters suggests a movie production company as the new model. It brings skilled people together who complete a focused project and then disband.

Know your rights and responsibilities as an independent contractor. Get a good tax adviser and financial planner. You probably won't be getting paid on the 1st and 15th of the month anymore.

6. Networking. Keep in touch with all your contacts, especially past employers and friends at major corporations. Know how to submit a request for proposal for subcontract work, which could be your lifeblood as a small business or independent contractor. Have a network of contacts across the country and keep touch with them. Refer business to them when you have an opportunity to do so.

7. Continued education. Take courses and teach. You will gain a reputation as an expert and become an acknowledged leader in your field—and keep on the cutting edge.

8. Sharpen your competitive edge. Find out what it is. If you speak well, do seminars. If you write well, write papers and articles. If you socialize well, go to networking events. If you synthesize well, publish a survey. Use your competitive edge as a spotlight for your dream career.

Management expert Peter F. Drucker has said, "The business enterprise has two—and only two—basic functions—marketing and innovation. Marketing and innovation produce results; all the rest are 'costs.' Learn how to market yourself, your expertise, skills and services."

Bottom line, no matter what the trends and soothsayers predict, if you plan to create your own business or change careers, it is your responsibility to spend time determining whether there will be customers and a place for your dream career in the new marketplace.

The pursuit of a dream career, for many people, is an exercise in living for today—for the first time in their lives. It is enjoying the process, and the path toward the dream as much as the goal and the benefits.

If you can't deal with frustration, don't go for your dream career—because chances are the experience will be filled with frustration, exhilaration and the great ups and downs that come with making massive changes in your life.

There is a Japanese proverb that says, "The reverse side also has a reverse side." If you're going for your dream career, you can certainly understand the meaning of that phrase: With the new comes something even newer—change and more change.

Homework

1. Consider the diversity of the work force and the impact of the global economy. Identify your international contacts as well as those friends and associates who represent different ethnic influences. What could you learn from these individuals that might help you launch your dream career? How could they assist you?

2. Identify the technoskills and technology that might improve your chances of success in your dream career—i.e., a new computer, better software, etc.

3. Do you know any retirees who could be interested in working with you on your dream career? Check out the SBAs (Small Business Administration) and the RSVP (Retired Senior Volunteer Program) for possible part-time workers.

4. Attend an upcoming computer fair to see what new equipment and technological services there are. Get names of people who may be good resources for your dream career.

5. Get the list of continuing education courses from your college/university to see what's missing. You might want to consider teaching a class in your area of expertise. It will build your credibility as well as lead you to new contacts.

6. Your skills, your career

1. What is your special talent—the one skill you're very proud of?

_____

_____

_____

_____

_____

2. List other special skills and talents you have.

_____

_____

_____

_____

3. List any skills you may need to attain to realize your dream career (learn a language, become familiar with computers).

_____

_____

_____

_____

4. How can you incorporate this special talent into your career?

_____

_____

_____

_____

5. If you could invent a new career, what would it be? How could technology help you?

_____

_____

_____

_____

6. How can you position yourself as an expert? Can you combine work you did with experience you've gained?

_____

_____

_____

_____

7. How can serendipity help your career? Can you make your own luck? Give three examples of how you've gotten "lucky."

_____

_____

_____

_____

_____

8. What is a high-tech job you'd like if you knew how to handle the equipment?

_____

_____

_____

_____

9. What's a high-touch career you'd like—something that you create with your hands, heart, etc?

_____

_____

_____

_____

_____

How to find your dream career

> "You are led through your lifetime by the inner learning creature, the playful spiritual being that is your real self. Don't turn away from possible futures before you're certain you don't have anything to learn from them. You're always free to change your mind and choose a different future, or a different past."
>
> —Illusions: The Adventures of a Reluctant Messiah, by Richard Bach (author of Jonathan Livingston Seagull)

What is it that so often keeps us mired in the muck of a go-nowhere job? Or causes us to hop from one job to the next—in perpetual pursuit of a better place? Often, career satisfaction escapes us because we haven't given any thought to what we love to do! We become experts on what aspects of our jobs we hate—long commute, low pay, tyrannical boss, boring work—but we avoid addressing what it is that really fulfills us.

Finding your "right livelihood"

The dream *is* possible. In the area of romance, many experts talk about the importance of finding your "soulmate."

In the area of work, the Buddhist concept of "right liveli-hood" refers to finding the work you were meant to do, do-ing it consciously and for others as well as yourself seems to best apply.

The opposite of "find" is "lose" and many of those people who come to me have lost their ability to dream. Is it any wonder they don't know what they really want to do. In my classes, I illustrate what it's like to lose the ability to dream. I take two balloons filled with helium and let one float to the ceiling. I start to let the helium out of the other balloon—first slowly and then more quickly. Sometimes so quickly I force it to pop loudly! Let the helium out of a balloon and it sounds like it's crying. Kind of like a person whose just been fired or one who is caught in the pressure cooker of life.

It's my belief that most people *do* know—somewhere in-side themselves—what they want to do or at least how they want to feel while realizing their dream. They want to be happy, they want to be challenged, they want to be children again and play at their work.

But something is stopping them.

What's stopping you from your dream?

There is an apocryphal story of Jack Benny, one of the great stars of early TV. Mr. Benny was invited to perform at the White House. He showed up at the gate with his violin case under his arm. A burly guard blocked his way. Somewhat tensely, the guard asked what was in the case. "A machine gun," he responded. The guard relaxed, "Oh, that's fine, Mr. Benny," he said. "Go right in. For a moment there I was afraid it was your violin."

Playing his violin was one of Jack Benny's great loves. And even though he didn't do it very well, he played it fre-quently on his nationally televised show. Despite the groans and protests from his audiences. But he played anyway. That's what living your dream is really about—staying true to what you want to do. Discovering your "right livelihood" and finding the work you were meant to do. Whether it is a standard career or something that you create yourself.

What will you be when you grow up?

As a child, you were probably asked a hundred times, if not more, "What are you going to be when you grow up?" Sometimes, the adults answered their own question. Aunt Louella would say, "He'll make a great policeman, like his dad," and Uncle Ted would run his hand through little Julie's hair and say, "She'll sure make some lucky guy a great wife some day." But what did you really want to do? Do you remember?

Some kids pick what their parents do. Others will rebel—like my client Al, who wanted to be a "car washer," since that seemed to be the guy who had more fun than his daddy who wore suits to work and complained about this person named "boss" all the time.

But most children do dream about how much freedom they'll have when they're "big." Freedom to drive a car, fly a plane or other things that would be possible if they were allowed into those hallowed grounds where "grown-ups" rule.

In the Hollywood movie "Big," directed by Penny Marshall and starring Tom Hanks, a 12-year-old wakes up in the body of a 30-year-old. And this child-man begins to charm the world around him with his sense of wonder and innocence and vitality for life.

From the mouth of babes...you can still rediscover that sense of passion you had about life as a kid. You can rekindle those childhood fantasies and dreams to help you discover the keys to your dream career.

What if you don't *know* what you want?

Those of you not sure what to do will want to follow every exercise in this section immediately. If you know where you're headed, you'll still want to package that with the "stardust" of your childhood experiences to ensure that you have the fuel to keep your dream burning brightly.

Time after time, I've asked Hollywood celebrities, politicians and athletes what is their secret to success, and they tell me it is one thing—the ability to look at the world with childlike wonder—to *play*, not work. To quote one of my past clients, acting coach Tracy Roberts, "Your goal is to be a child again."

An accident of fate

In researching this book, I asked many people how they knew what they wanted to become. How did they select their new life path? The most common answer? "It happened by accident." "I just fell into it." Yet in digging deeper, I have found repeatedly that there was some symmetry to the new career or lifestyle choice.

John said he never had the guts to start his own business. But suddenly it looked like he was going to get custody of his teen-age son so he rented a two-bedroom condo. When his son decided to continue living with his mother, John was devastated—but since he had the extra room he turned it into an office. Since he had to keep his mind occupied, he began his new business on nights and weekends. He turned the setback into a step forward. And now, three years later he has a thriving computer consulting business.

Moving from financial loss to career gain

Sometimes a financial loss can spur a person on to find his or her dream.

Karen and her husband, Bill, invested in a moneymaking venture—wholesale jewelry. They were just going to sit back and make money while the wholesaler opened retail stores throughout the West. Tragically, the fraud took their $10,000 and left them holding only boxes of costume jewelry. Karen, who was working as an insurance salesperson, was devastated. Bill, though, saw the bright side. He urged Karen to quit her job and sell the jewelry at flea markets—after all, if she could sell insurance in a down market she could certainly sell discount jewelry. Five years later, Karen is still selling jewelry at street fairs. Now, it is hand-crafted jewelry from artists she discovers as she travels across the country. She makes about half of what she made before—but she loves it.

Many of my clients have turned personal tragedy into triumph in living out their dreams. One of my favorite syndicated columnists, Ellen Goodman, has explained this phenomenon. "Our lives are littered with mid-course corrections. A full half of us divorced. Many of the women have had career paths that look like games of "Chutes and Ladders." We have changed directions and priorities again and again. But our 'mistakes' become crucial parts, sometimes the best parts, of the lives we have made."

In helping others, we help ourselves

There is often a certain serendipity involved in finding your dream. Many times something good or bad happens that influences you to pursue your dream. Sometimes it is something affecting someone dear to us and we want to help.

Entrepreneur James Shanahan tells the story in *Success* magazine, October 1992, of why he started "Hooked on Phonics," the creative musical book and audio program that teaches people to read—now an $85 million company. Shanahan had a problem many parents face—his son couldn't read. According to Shanahan (who used his background as an advertising copywriter and his education at the Phil Saltman School of Music in Boston), he decided to write and tape a little rhythmic song to teach him the sounds. In less than two months, his son was reading above his grade level. And then the neighbors said that their children were having trouble. Could he lend them the tapes?

In Shanahan's case it wasn't just the concept, it was the marketing, too. How can you forget his order number—1-800-ABCDEFG? To start his company Shanahan called that number and a man answered—he asked the man if he'd let him have the number—the man said no. Shanahan offered him $10,000 and the man said yes. "A lot of our initial success was due to that phone number," Shanahan explains.

Discovering the dream sometimes just happens. Turning it into a business involves savvy, guts and marketing expertise.

Time and again my clients tell me that they began their career after a tragic event—a car accident, a loss of money, being fired—changed their lives. Melody Beattie wrote *Codependent No More*, the book that started the 12-step movement, while she was on welfare.

Many of my clients derive inspiration from the Chinese ideogram for the word "crisis"—which also stands for "opportunity." Along the way, though, there will be challenges. That is when I encourage my clients to have faith.

For it is true that the process of recareering is akin to a the cycle of metamorphosis of a butterfly—moving from pupa to caterpillar to chrysalis to butterfly. And when the monarch is still and flightless in its crystal shell—that is when you must trust that it will be able to break out to dot our skies with wonder. Many of my clients say to me, "All you had to do was to reassure me that I would find my dream and then I believed—and I did."

Look for signs—and miracles

Psychotherapist Thomas Moore observes in his best seller *The Care of the Soul* that "Soul cannot thrive in a fast-paced life because being affected, taking things in and chewing on them, requires time. Living artfully, therefore, might require something as simple as pausing. Some people are incapable of being arrested by things because they are always on the move."

So if it doesn't seem like it's "fitting together," if it seems like everything, in fact, is falling apart—you may indeed be on the right track. You may, in picking up the pieces, discover a part of the puzzle you never noticed before.

How are dream career makers sure they are moving ahead? Sometimes there are signs—visible or almost mystical in nature. You meet someone who went to your grade school who's now in the career you've been thinking about. Your next-door neighbor wants to introduce you to the guy who just bought the bank. A celebrity uses your security guard services and offers you a job running his company. Your car breaks down in a small town and you decide to stay to run the diner.

Astrologer Joan Levin of Sedona, Arizona, told me, "If something happens once notice it, if something happens twice look closer, if it happens three times—wake up and follow that direction." I encourage my clients to look to the past, to the present and, yes, to the future. I advise my clients to ask for a sign that indicates they are on the right track. It doesn't have to be big—it doesn't have to be like a pie in your face. It can be a book on gardening that falls off the shelf in the library at your feet. It can be an old computer that someone offers to give you—or a chance to house-sit for a neighbor's aunt in Norway. Expect the unexpected. Invite the new, the unusual.

Many times, I go even further and tell my clients to *ask* for a miracle. Something that will show them they are on the right track. Even a metaphysical sign. (You think it's weird? Didn't you ever follow the North Star when you were lost?)

Some clients look to their dreams for signs. Screenwriters say that their stories sometimes come from their dreams. One inventor I worked with said that his exercise equipment (now featured on a national infomercial) was first demonstrated to him in his dreams. Other times, clients discover half-hearted projects they once tinkered on 20 years ago in the backs of their garages. Others find an uncompleted medical-school application in an old trunk left from college dorm days and realize that they gave up on their real dream.

How to become a "kid" again

Take a moment and think about your childhood dreams. If you want you can use a formal visualization technique like "Creative Visualization" by Shakti Gawain, which may help you to use your imagination to create what you want in your life, or "Applied Visualization," a mind-body program by James Lynn Page.

Or you can look through your photo albums and pull out a photo of you as a child and imagine what that child valued, what he or she got excited about.

To recreate the feeling of what you loved doing as a child, get in the mood by remembering your favorite childhood "outfit."

Mark remembers his cowboy outfit with hat, chaps, vest and holster with toy guns. He even slept in it for a few days after he got it for a birthday. No, he didn't grow up to be a cowboy, but he did grow up to do his own thing—to explore the wide-open spaces of life as a musician, martial artist, writer and entrepreneur. In that outfit, he felt in charge. After all he was the sheriff of his life—not Mom or Dad—and he had a badge to prove it.

Think about your favorite childhood outfit. Was it a Halloween costume? Or clown pajamas? A frilly dress that made you feel like a princess? A firefighter's hat?

The very best way to rediscover the dream is to become a kid again. No, not like in the movie, "Big." But roll up your pants, kick off your shoes and go somewhere for a day, a week or a weekend where you can just run and play. It's not as easy as it sounds. Some of my clients say it takes them two or three days or a week to wind down.

Here are some typical kid-time activities.

Spend a day at the park. Pack a lunch—peanut butter and jelly or some fun lunch that you remember. Yes, even potato chip sandwiches are OK. But *pack* one—don't stop at the deli or fast-food place. Bring your favorite childhood drink (nonalcoholic, please). Mine was grapefruit juice from the can served at my nursery school.

Take a kite, grab a ball or some childhood toy or game like "jacks." Try to leave your wallet and your purse at home so you're not burdened by adult responsibilities. Afterward, sit in your car or the bus or the subway on the way home and jot some notes in a notebook or diary about how it felt to be playing again.

Think about how you can translate some of those feelings of excitement or contentment into your new career and into your chosen lifestyle of the future.

Take lessons. Ballet, soccer, skating, clarinet or swimming. Whether you took lessons as a kid, or always wanted to, it's never too late! I took tap as a kid and almost cried the first time I went back as an adult. First, I had forgotten how hard it was and, second, I was so proud when the teacher, a trained Broadway dancer, said I must have been adorable as a little girl.

For me, tap meant fun and excitement and the chance to dance my way to fame and fortune. Unfortunately, I didn't have the option of continuing, and baton twirling didn't lead to a career. But later in life, I did share my interest in tap with Robert Redford when I met him at his Sundance Institute in Utah. He had just danced in the movie "Legal Eagles." We both chatted and he thanked that "now anonymous tap-dancing teacher" in Navy Park's housing project for turning me on to the excitement of "shuffle/clog and life."

It's not that important what you choose to do, what really matters is to somehow recreate that thrill you had as a child. Can you feel that sense of fancy now? If so, what was it like?

During this experience, some of my clients reflame a long-forgotten passion. They may choose to pursue dancing or music or sports as a career. And I say—*do it!* Most career counselors dismiss these pipe dreams. Well, sure you can't expect to dance the lead in "Swan Lake" if you just started ballet lessons at 40. But you might pursue a job doing accounting or promoting your local ballet company.

The choice is yours. You can "play" baseball for $5,000 one week a year at an exclusive spring training camp, or you can move to a minor league city and get a job as controller for the team. Or, you may choose to stay at your old J.O.B., but give up your country club membership for box seats at Anaheim stadium.

The only thing about being an adult is that if you want your dream career—you have to be brave enough to make the choices. Some people talk the talk but don't walk the walk. They get so caught up in the "plan" that they hesitate to take the "trip."

Turning your life around

If you're still stuck, here's a list of dream careers that my students and clients are now living:

- Judy Kerr was a housewife who became an acting coach and actor at 50.
- Cathryn Michon, an actress who used to be with Second City in Chicago, is now the story editor for the TV show "Designing Women."
- Charlene Thorburn, an RN, is now a chiropractor.
- Jeffrey Armstrong, a former computer executive, is now the world's first "high-tech comedian."
- Lena Moszkowski switched from real estate entrepreneur to barrio teacher at age 30. Now in her 60s, she's switched to author and speaker calling for educational reform.

Other clients have switched from sales to law, from law to retail store owner, from actor to fine artist, from eyeglass salesman to TV talk show host, from banker to teacher. There are no limits.

Most of my really successful clients invent or reinvent traditional jobs/careers and customize them to fit their talents. Susan, a community activist, realized that she wanted to be a lawyer but couldn't stand wearing a suit and working in an office. Today, she operates a storefront law practice in East L.A. and she thrives on the excitement of working with the residents who are building a better community for their children.

You're never too old to live your dream

Age is no excuse either. Many people start their dream ventures at an older age.

- Sol Price started the Price Club at 60.
- Ray Kroc started McDonalds at 52.
- Karl Eller became CEO of Circle supermarkets at 50.
- Julia Child, now 80, took her first bite of French food at 37 and started her TV career in her 50s.
- Millicent Fenwick won her first race for Congress at 65.
- William Shakespeare switched from writing comedies to tragedies in his late 30s.
- Paul Gauguin, a Paris stockbroker until 35, left for Tahiti at 45.

You may find, like many of my clients who've struggled to discover their true dream career, that what you really need now is time. Time to rediscover who you are and what you love to do. Time to explore and test and sample many experiences. Time to contemplate and sort out and identify your feelings.

If you're under pressure to pay the mortgage or to keep peace in the household by getting a J.O.B., remember: This is *your* life! As far as we all know, you only get one. If you're not certain what is important to you, you may not be able to live out your real dream.

In his book, *Live and Learn and Pass It On*, H. Jackson Brown Jr. includes words of wisdom from people age 5 to 95. I share some of the comments from the senior citizens:

"I've learned that deciding whom you marry is the most important decision you'll ever make." Age 95.

"I've learned you shouldn't compare yourself to the best others do, but to the best you can do." Age 68.

"I've learned that good advice is hard to give, but even harder to follow." Age 68.

"I've learned that nothing of value comes without effort." Age 64.

"I've learned that kindness is more important than perfection." Age 70.

"I've learned that education, experience and memories are three things that no one can take away from you." Age 67.

Going for your dream career means doing it in spite of the odds, in spite of what others think and in spite of the chunk that may come from your own wallet.

My client Donald Cayea was a successful insurance lawyer who yearned to go into entertainment law and to produce movies, too. To live his dream, he chose to leave his firm and form his own partnership with understanding and supportive partners who respected his goals. He launched himself into the arena of entertainment by speaking at film festivals while he was still building up his entertainment client base.

During the writing of this book he contacted me to tell me that the first "off-off Broadway" musical was receiving rave reviews. He's optioned several film projects and is starting to make some great deals. Is he getting super-rich? Not yet, he reports. But he says, "I've sacrificed some income—yes, maybe lots of income, but I love this and the crowds clapping. And the excitement the cast shows on their faces after the musical is a bigger payoff than I could have ever anticipated."

Finding soul-satisfying work, finding your reason for being is the most exciting thing you can do in life. For when you discover it, everything else seems in sync. But recareering is a process, not a set plan. It involves a series of seven cycles:

1. Breaking from the past. From your family, from the expectations of others, from your failures, from your own overdemanding expectations.

2. Rediscovering your sense of childhood wonder. Rekindling that sense of awe, of being happy to wake up in the morning. Of loving to play at what you do. Of wanting to do it so badly that you'd do it even if you weren't paid.

3. Sorting out what you do best. What are your special gifts? How can you make a contribution to the world? What is the legacy you can leave behind?

4. Creating your own "right livelihood." Having the guts to play your violin. Really creating, not just choosing, not just studying, not just doing—but creating something so special that it feels like you were just meant to do this.

5. Researching and developing the dream. Testing it out, experiencing it for a day, a week, a few months. Revising it to fit *you*. Getting some additional education.

6. Living the dream. Going for your personal best, despite what people say, despite how afraid you may be. Despite the figure in your bank account. Nurturing yourself along the way—taking care of mind and body and soul so that, like a rocket, you don't burn out along the course to your personal stardom.

7. Building a bridge beyond. The dream must lead you to more. It is an ongoing adventure, not just a destination. What are you going to do when you're a lawyer? How can you make a contribution as just another social worker in an overworked system? How can you deal with the frustration of teaching in an inner city school? Your destiny is built of many dreams. And you get to design them all.

But what if the timing's not right for you to venture off on your dream career? What if you can't afford to take time off from your job? What if your family pressures are too intense and you feel boxed in? I suggest you just forget about your dream career for now—*really*! And head for your local video store. You have my permission to just "veg out."

Just do yourself one last favor. Pick up any one of these films, too, because they may push you back on your course to your dream career. After all, why did you buy this book? To get another 9-to-5 job?

"Field of Dreams." Adapted from a novel by W.P. Kinsella called *Shoeless Joe*. This film has inspired many to create their own fields of dreams.

"Auntie Mame." A favorite of mine. Remember her famous line "Life is a banquet and some poor sons of bitches are starving"?

"The Wizard of Oz." Trust that *your* Oz is out there, and it doesn't take a cyclone to send you to find it.

"Rocky." Knowing that Sly Stallone bet his future on this picture may inspire you to move forward.

"The Miracle Worker." Helen Keller said, "Life is either a daring adventure or nothing."

"Chariots of Fire." Can you run the distance in your own personal Olympics?

"The Milagro Beanfield War." The little guy against the odds, and those wonderful angels who come to help—almost magical.

"Lorenzo's Oil." You *can* beat the system—even if you don't have a medical degree, or a film degree or a law degree...

Enjoy the trip along the way. As one my favorite film characters, Buckaroo Bonzai, in the same-named cult classic says, "Remember, wherever you go, there you are!"

Homework

1. Go to your local library—head straight for the kids' section. Pull out some books and begin reading randomly, try to rekindle that sense of childhood wonder.
2. Revitalize your spiritual side—go to church or synagogue or read some Zen philosophy or whatever gives you a sense that you are more than just body and mind.
3. Buy yourself something you always wanted as a kid—a 10-speed bike, a Yankees baseball cap, patent leather shoes. Treat yourself well—you're special.

7. Reliving your childhood dreams

1. What's the earliest thing you remember wanting to do when you grew up (drive a car, make money, wear pretty dresses, etc.)?

_____

_____

_____

2. When people asked you what you wanted to do when you were grown up, what did you say?

_____

_____

_____

How did you feel when they asked you?

_____

_____

_____

3. What did you want to do as a little kid that you haven't done yet? (list three things)

_____

_____

_____

4. What childhood dreams have you accomplished? (List as many as you can remember.)

_____

_____

_____

_____

_____

_____

5. Why did/didn't you want to do what your parents did for a living?

_____

_____

_____

6. What games did you most enjoy?

_____

_____

_____

_____

7. What did you excel at?

_____

_____

8. What did you love, but were not good at?

_____

_____

9. What lessons did you take? How did you feel about those lessons?

_____

_____

_____

10. What did you learn about "team playing" from athletics?

_____

_____

_____

11. Did you ever win an award for your prowess in athletics or in academics?

_____

_____

_____

12. Were you ever the best in your class at anything? If so, what was it?

_____

_____

_____

_____

13. What do you still enjoy doing for recreation that you did as a kid?

_____

_____

_____

_____

14. Describe a favorite photo of yourself as a kid.

_____

_____

_____

_____

15. What was your favorite childhood outfit and why?

_____

_____

_____

_____

16. As a kid, which would you have preferred to do, and why?

❏ Go to the park   ❏ Have a pajama party
❏ Go to the zoo   ❏ Travel to Europe
❏ Play baseball   ❏ Travel to Disneyland

_____

_____

_____

_____

Personal values and your dream career

"You don't get to choose how you're going to die. Or when. You can only decide how you're going to live. Now."

—Joan Baez

So just what is the secret to finding your dream career? I can almost guarantee you that you can successfully recareer if you are *value-driven* rather than money-driven. Packaging your career with your personality and personal values is a relatively new concept. One that I have found has dramatically increased the odds of finding a fulfilling career for my thousands of clients.

For five decades, since the end of World War II, Americans have been influenced to choose their jobs by the offerings of the marketplace, the recommendations of their high school or college career counselors, their scores on standardized aptitude tests and their financial demands and goals. Success was measured by salary, job title, perks and benefits packages.

When I've asked my clients who were trying to escape careers in law, medicine or engineering why they originally pursued such courses, I've invariably received the same response: "Because it paid well and there was a big demand." But here they were, despite the attractive paycheck and job security, desperate to leave the stresses and "bad fit" they'd suffered. Sometimes it only took a day, sometimes it took a few years to realize, "The job really isn't me."

Studies by Dr. Cary Cherniss of both professionals and nonprofessionals indicate that an individual can report high job satisfaction at the same time he feels alienated from his work. Quite an odd response, which becomes understandable when you discover that many people no longer expect much from their work. They are satisfied because they are getting as much from their work as they expect—and their expectations aren't high. Instead they find payoffs in money, status, recognition, names on the door and private bathrooms.

As author John Dos Passos has said, "People don't choose their careers, they are engulfed by them." Workaholism was the norm in the '80s. For example, lawyers and other professionals were often evaluated by how many billable hours they could charge back to their clients rather than by the work itself.

Psychotherapist Thomas Moore says:

"It's obvious that climbing the ladder of success can easily lead to a loss of soul. An alternative may be to choose a profession or projects with soul in mind. If a potential employer describes the benefits of a job, we could ask about the soul values. What is the spirit of this workplace? Will I be treated as a person here? Is what we are doing and producing worthy of my commitment and long hours? Are there any moral problems in the job or workplace—making things detrimental to people or to the earth, taking excessive profits or contributing to racial and sexual oppression? It is not possible to care for the soul while violating or disregarding one's own moral sensibility."

85

I encourage you to look closely at your career experience and to recreate not only your career but your whole attitude toward work. To create based on your skills, your personality and your personal values and on the contribution you can offer to help make a better world for all of us.

In the past, if the going got rough and you started to hate your work, your boss or your new assignment, there was always an option—*quit* and find another job. After all, you were experienced. Or if you were a union member—you could always file a grievance. For many people, the system protected us only *en masse*. Our individualism, our creativity and our personal values were spindled and folded like computer cards of yesteryear to fit the company mold.

Even what we wore was mandated by the corporate rules and regulations—from the advertising man's gray flannel to the secretary's requisite white gloves and hat of the 1950s to the Big Blue (IBM) "uniform" of white shirts and blue pinstripes to the requisite "new woman's" uniform of bow ties and blazers.

Suddenly, the recession hit and the working world changed. But with all the bad came some good. A new emphasis on personal fulfillment, which many of you are now exploring, evolved.

Books like *Do What You Love, The Money Will Follow* (by Marsha Sinetar) have gone mainstream. Words like *visualization* and *manifestation* (being able to create what you want) are fast becoming buzzwords in the corporate world where *job enrichment* and *quality circles* are creating new styles of management—for a new kind of employee.

A new era of entrepreneurism and *intrapreneurism* (acting like an entrepreneur within a company structure) has been launched. And more than ever before, we are looking not just at the bottom line, but the meaning and satisfaction we will find in our work.

Value-driven career choices count

That's why I am a true believer in value-driven career selection. Beverly Kaye, author of *Invest in Your Values*, says, "Finding satisfaction in your work can contribute to your long-term happiness, and even your health. As success is being reevaluated in the '90s, many people are finding that more is no longer the answer. Some individuals are reaching for quality to replace quantity. They are finding that a match between their values and their work produces fulfillment."

Did your high school or college counselor ever ask you what was more important to you—freedom or power? Did a boss ever care about how exciting you found your work?

Newspaper mogul Katherine Graham sums up the new philosophy of work in the '90s by saying, "To love what you do and feel that it matters—how could anything be more fun?"

The forces that should drive you should be internal, not external. Your destination should be determined by your personality and your personal values.

Easy to say, right? Tough to do? *Yes.*

But to achieve your dreams, you must stay true to *you*. They wanted Barbra Streisand to change her nose. They wanted Hillary Rodham Clinton to change her clothes. They wanted Arnold Schwarzenegger to change his name. But these accomplished and much-admired individuals stayed true to themselves.

Take the test on the next page to see what is most important to you at this point in your life. Identify 10 values that are most significant to you and prioritize them from 1 (most important) to 10. Following are examples of some values you might consider:

Recognition	Reputation
Security	Acknowledgment
Money	Freedom
Family	Spirituality
Friends	Honesty
Excitement	Environment
Power	Respect

Now consider which, if any, values play into your career as it is now. For example, let's say you selected freedom, excitement and environment as your top three values. Your work on the assembly line at a plastics factory is clearly in conflict with your values.

Then, you can use your values to help guide you in choosing your dream career. Freedom, excitement and environment, say, might stimulate thoughts of an outdoor career—possibly running your own whitewater tour company.

Now, take a moment and answer this question: What would you do if you were given $1 million dollars right now? Allocate the $1 million among the 10 actions you'd take.

1. _____   6. _____
2. _____   7. _____
3. _____   8. _____
4. _____   9. _____
5. _____   10. _____

Kathy, a successful actress/producer who landed her own production company and TV series before she was 30, came to me after she had failed to launch another TV series. Now, she wanted to sell a screenplay that featured her in the lead. She seemed to lack passion for the project, so I asked her to take the "Million Dollar Quiz." Here were her top choices:

1. Go to Tahiti.
2. Have a child.
3. Buy a mountain retreat.
4. Invest in real estate.
5. Paint in my own studio.

Her screenplay project was not even included on the list. By analyzing Kathy's choices, we decided that she'd be best pursuing another project of hers—a children's travelogue series for a major cable network. If the project proved successful, it would give her more payoffs than the film. She would have time to pursue a personal life, have a child and do oil painting while her residuals flowed in.

To help you determine how your personality and personal values fit with your prospective dream career, look at this sampling of typical personality traits linked to specific careers. There are always exceptions, of course—shy salespeople and gregarious seamstresses. But the list will give you some idea of how certain professions tend to lend themselves to certain personality types.

These examples are based on my work with more than 2,000 individuals in more than 200 careers. Remember, there are exceptions to every rule. And you can be that exception and still triumph in your dream career.

Costume designers. Innovators, resourceful, relentless, strong sense of color and design. Ability to take direction and deal with high levels of frustration and change. Excellent business sense. Flamboyant and highly verbal.

Restaurant owners. Pioneers, excellent cooks—or food lovers, great organizers, extremely high energy level, detail-oriented. Often volatile and charismatic. Thrive on client appreciation and celebrity recognition.

Psychologists, therapists. Helpers and leaders who handle crises well. Thrive on intensity and are able to nourish themselves emotionally so that they don't burn out. Frequently great talkers, and can be quite personable and charismatic.

Mimes/comedians. Performers who love to make people smile. Charismatic, not embarrassed easily, persevere against all odds. Thick-skinned and able to bounce back after failure.

Athletes. Achievers. Seek recognition, but they are driven by the score—their goal is to stand out from the crowd. The "retiring" team member is an exception. Athletes must be able to perform as team players—whether or not they enjoy sharing the spotlight.

Chiropractors. Encouragers and great analysts. Able to deal with high levels of frustration. People-oriented.

Nurses. Good team players. Self starters. Caring. Detail-oriented. Thorough. Able to deal with high levels of stress.

Magazine editors. Good perspective, good trend spotters. Great computer skills. Multiple interests. Good writing and editing skills. Diplomatic.

Social workers. Patient. Great research skills. Belief in the basic good nature of people. Desire to make a difference. Community-oriented. Reliable and trust-worthy. Good communicator.

Artists. Independent, enjoy challenging the status quo. Like to work on own terms. Demand high personal freedom. Relish being different from the masses. Mavericks.

Adapting the career to you

Now let's answer your question about what if your personality doesn't fit the "norm" for a certain profession.

What if you want to be an artist but need structure and a predictable income? You may want to apply for a grant. You may want to work as a graphic artist in an advertising agency. You may want to work in an art gallery during the day and paint on weekends. My suggestion is to get as close to your dream as you can. For example, at the ad agency you may have an opportunity to use your illustrations for an ad if you keep pitching them. You may meet a copywriter who wants to join you in writing your book.

What if you want to be a nurse but find that you're not a particularly nurturing person? You may want to choose to work in medical research. If you want more independence, you may choose private-care nursing.

Thus, you're adapting the job to fit your personality. This is an area where you can't compromise. You have to analyze your skills and your interests very carefully so that in your excitement to cash another paycheck, you don't get caught up in a system that doesn't care about you and your goals.

The best personality trait

My clients frequently ask me, "If I could develop one personality trait that would guarantee my success, what would it be?" I wish I could say that all successful people were warm or caring or loving or honest or leaders or great bosses. But, consistently, there is only one trait that I find that all of my successful dream career makers have: an unerring sense that they are doing the right thing.

Not that they don't have self-doubt some of the time. Jane Fonda reflects on her own self-doubt: "Sometimes I think I'm the luckiest person in the world. There's nothing better than having work you care about. Sometimes I think my greatest problem is lack of confidence. I'm scared and I think that's healthy." Fonda moves right through her fear to accomplish her goals personally and professionally.

So although successful career makers may have doubts, they work these out. To the outside world, they project a strong sense of confidence, satisfaction and direction. After all, you wouldn't want to buy a Chrysler from Lee Iacocca if he said, "Well, I'm thinking about how, maybe, I haven't done such a good job in my business or my career."

How to prepare for the big time

Clients frequently ask me what they should do while preparing to make a transition. How can they endure their jobs? Instead of just focusing on the future, I encourage them to live each day to its fullest, to begin to adapt their jobs to their personalities.

Maybe you'll want to see if you can make some trades. For example, if your job involves public speaking and you know this is not your forte, perhaps you can develop a video. Then, all you have to do is introduce the video and close the presentation. Or perhaps you can record a cassette.

If you like an unstructured environment and the work-style is very structured, you may want to use your breaks and your lunch time for personally fulfilling activities, whether volleyball, reading, workouts or museum-going. Take a break and close your door—stand on our head, do yoga or play your walkman.

Many times, relieving stress in your current environment is key in helping you pursue your dream career. Here are some great ways to relieve stress, courtesy of my client Krs Edstrom, author of the book, *Conquering Stress.* Edstrom is a health-style consultant who organizes corporate wellness programs for clients such as Universal Studios. She suggests that you develop both external and internal skills to deal with the stress during your transition. Her external skill suggestions include:

1. Get a simple time management book.

2. Develop money management skills.

3. Learn how to set boundaries in your life.

4. Develop an interest in "touch therapy." Encourage your pals and loved ones to give you neck and shoulder massages and return the favors.

5. Develop a creative outlet—a diversion such as photography or stamp collecting. (Even if you want to spend every minute on your new career, it's important to balance that drive with another outlet.)

Some internal skills Edstrom suggests are learning to breath deeply and exploring meditation and visualization. If the going gets really rough, Edstrom says, grab your pillow and start screaming! Yes, *scream* at the top of your lungs. If you're working at your J.O.B. and it's just too much, slip out for a few minutes, run around the block or up and down the stairs.

Take care that you don't eat foods that are aggravating to your stress levels—especially sugar, caffeine or foods that you're sensitive to. Be sure to exercise three times a week. Yes, even if it's just 20 to 30 minutes. Edstrom says make sure your exercise is not partner-oriented. Then you'll have no excuses. No money to join a gym? Check out ESPN television's "Body Shapers" televised twice a day. Tape a few episodes and you'll have your own exercise videos. Or pretend you're a kid again and use a jump rope in your backyard to benefit from some quick aerobics. Just be sure that your exercise program is excuse-proof, low-cost, easy to do and *fun*.

High energy is one of the common denominators of successful people. A good night's rest is crucial. Actor/producer Robert Townsend says, "You can't hang around with the crew drinking beer after the day's shoot, you have to be refreshed and need time for your mind to regenerate." Good advice. Even the friendliest people start to snap at fellow workers and family when they're exhausted.

Nurture yourself with your values in mind

When we're not fulfilled in our careers or other aspects of our lives, we often seek releases—food, alcohol, smoking, partying too late—that aggravate our state of anxiety even further. On the journey toward your dream career, remember to nurture yourself—in ways that are good for you and are in sync with your values. Say you're currently juggling work and school in a congested metropolitan area, with a long-term goal of moving to a rural area. You can treat yourself to weekend drives in the country—bring your books with you and study in the peace of a rolling field.

Think about your own personality and values when you need special care. Stressful day on the J.O.B.? If you're a person who thrives on "alone" time, you'd do better to plan an evening at home with a stack of your favorite magazines and steaming bubblebath rather than a night on the town at a noisy bar with friends.

Throughout the recareering process, and for that matter, throughout your life, it's important that you have an intimate relationship with your personal values and make sure that they're reflected in your work. A career in conflict with these values will result in painful discord at the very least. Tuning your career to your values will create a satisfying harmony.

Homework

1. Make a list of the 10 most important personal values to you (see samples of values on page 88.)
2. Prioritize those values in order of importance to you.
3. Identify which values you've had a chance to implement in past jobs or careers. For example, if power is important to you, examine your work history for situations in which you supervised others, made decisions and had significant responsibility. Evaluate how satisfying these experiences were.
4. Identify which values you've *not* been able to incorporate in past jobs or careers. For example, family may be important to you, but your jobs may have required lots of overtime and travel.
5. Think about activities you enjoy—not necessarily activities you've carried out in a job. And see if you can identify at least one of your personal values that is tied to it. For example, you love to cook and entertain. Perhaps you listed time with friends and family as an important value.

---

8. The dream career map: How to get from here to there

Start: What are you doing now?

_____
_____
_____

Goal: What is your career goal?

_____
_____
_____

Getting on the road to the dream

1. What can you read about your career (trade magazines, reference books, professional brochures, textbooks, etc.)?

_____
_____

2. How much money will you need along the way? Check with accountants, professional contacts and outside sources like the SBA or the local Economic Development Councils.

_____
_____

3. How can you see your dream in action (observing others on the job, etc.)?

_____
_____
_____
_____

4. What are the names of the professional groups for your dream career? Check the *Directory of Associations* and other reference books.

_____

_____

_____

_____

5. What classes/courses will help you toward your goal (local extension programs, trade institutes for specialized adult programs, etc.)?

_____

_____

_____

_____

6. How can you experience you dream along the way (volunteer activities, apprenticeships, etc.)?

_____

_____

_____

_____

_____

7. Who do you know who can help along the way (accountants, lawyers, restaurant owners where you use your Platinum American Express card, etc.)?

_____

_____

_____

_____

8. On a separate sheet of paper, write a visual picture of you in your dream career. Describe where you would work, how you'd look, how you'd feel.

9. Packaging yourself for success

At the recent National Cable Television Association conference in San Francisco, Keith Howes, Director or Training for Continental Television noted that the Department of Labor and the American Society for Training and Development identified basic skills crucial to success in the workplace.

Basics

_____Ability to learn

_____Reading/writing

_____Computation

_____Oral communication

_____Good listening

_____Resourcefulness

_____Creative thinking

_____Self-esteem

_____Motivation

_____Goal-setting

_____Ability to plan for tomorrow (career development)

_____Interpersonal skills

_____Teamwork

_____Negotiation

_____Understanding organized culture

_____Shared leadership

Make sure you have these basics covered and then check how many of the following personal skills you bring to your new career.

Others

_____Sense of color	_____Good at numbers
_____Organized	_____Creative
_____High energy	_____Good with children
_____Good at details	_____Patient
_____Handle crisis well	_____Charismatic
_____Great talker	_____Computer literate
_____Good public speaker	_____Adventurous
_____Sense of humor	_____Good manager
_____Clever	_____Bilingual/multilingual
_____Witty	_____Good report writer
_____Team player	_____Thorough
_____Leader	_____Intuitive
_____Innovator	_____Lots of endurance
_____Good analyzer	_____Self-starter
_____Pioneer	_____Flexible
_____Thick-skinned	_____Inspirational
_____Good at dealing with change	_____Methodical

Get a life, not just a job

"To change one's life: start immediately, do it flamboyantly. No exceptions."

William James

As you determine the course of your career path, you'll discover that other facets of your life will enter into the picture as well—where you live, how you spend your money, how you spend your free time. This career-planning time is also time to think about *life* planning. When I meet with my clients for the first time, before I ask them what they want to *do*, I ask them what kind of life they want to live.

Even in carefree Hawaii, there's an expression—*Pau Hana*—meaning "after work." Until the last decade, most of our lives were built around *work* and *after work*. It always seemed upside-down to me that our society encourages us to work long hours at something we may hate in order to get a few hours to do something we really love. When I grew up in the Midwest, it was the highest of compliments to be referred to as a good worker or a hard worker.

Our days are typically divided into getting ready for work, going to work, working, working lunches, working late, going home from work, dinner and doing the work we took home to do and then planning for the next day of work.

And so day in and day out, 50 weeks a year with two weeks off, we follow this cycle. And we join—you guessed it—the "rat race" until we are so worn out that we have to be retired.

We have retirement planners and financial planners but few of us have ever met a *lifestyle planner*.

As we've already discussed, you'll probably have as many as seven careers (or more) in your lifetime. As my mom said so succinctly when I told her the title of this book, "Yes, no more one job." If you are value-driven and lifestyle-driven, you'll find it much easier to create a rewarding career when it fits with your lifestyle.

Integrate your life/work choice

Just remember, this time you're not starting over—you're starting *better*. In writing this chapter, I wanted to include spectacular stories of people who would inspire you to believe that you could trade your necktie for a lasso and ride the open range or sell your Jaguar and spend the next season of your life climbing Mt. Everest. Here are three examples of how people not only changed careers but integrated their career choices into their lives:

I had the good fortune to work with baseball hero Sadaharu Oh, "the Japanese Babe Ruth." Oh San, as he is called, retired from baseball and yearned to give back to the people some of the joy of the game he had so loved. It was my honor to work with him to set up the World Children's Baseball Foundation, a camp where kids around the world meet to play ball for a few weeks each year. By sharing what he loved, he created a new career for himself in the process. But he didn't do it alone. I worked with him to create a board of advisers ranging from Hollywood celebrities to business leaders to other athletes to help make his dream come true. Now he can travel around the world each summer visiting his baseball camps in foreign lands.

Another extraordinary man was already integrating his career with his lifestyle in his 20s. I met Douglas Heir while working with Olympians Mary Lou Retton and Bob Richards on the Wheaties Search for Champions—a national quest for outstanding amateur athletes. Heir was a member of the U.S. Olympic team wheelchair division. He won four medals at the World Olympic Wheelchair games in the javelin and discus competitions. At the time I met him, Heir was also a law student and teaching assistant at Rutgers University.

Gina, another client, discovered that her true calling was in social work. "There is nothing more fulfilling than helping to build a community center brick by brick, board by board with your own hands," she explains. A stint as a volunteer on a local crisis line led her to go back to school at 35 to get her master's degree in social work. Through an internship she realized that just the schooling would not be enough to change her lifestyle. She had to find a place where her one-on-one counseling would change lives. A grant allowed her to establish a shelter for battered women.

Too old to change your life?

Many people worry that they are too old to start over. Yet, I've found that my clients successfully recareer at all ages. San Francisco actor and writer Dean Goodman dreamed his whole life of doing films and, in his 70s, broke in as a co-star in Francis Ford Coppola's movie "Tucker."

In doing research for this book, I came across an interesting fact about illustrator H.A. Rey, noted for his charming drawings of Curious George, the nosey little monkey who is always getting himself in and out of trouble.

Rey, who lived from 1898 to 1977, sold bathtubs up and down the Amazon River from the age of 26 to 38 until he married his wife, Margaret. Then he embarked on an artistic career that produced Curious George. From bathtub salesman on the Amazon to children's book illustrator. Quite a lifestyle change.

Life changes brought on by crisis

Not all career changes are planned. Many start by accident or when people like you and me go through tough times—divorce, termination, financial crisis.

Actor Ed O'Neil, who plays Al Bundy on the television show "Married With Children," was a professional football player at one time. After being cut from the pro team, he decided to take a break (like many of my clients do) and stay in Florida where he had been in spring training. He supported himself as a bellboy at the same hotel he had stayed as a ballplayer.

He needed what I call a "station break" in life. This is not an easy time for most of my clients. And in fact, making a transition is often filled with a potpourri of emotions—confusion, anger, regret and hope. And challenges. As a bellboy, O'Neil was called to the front desk one day to carry the bags of some of his former team members who were back in town to play football. Can you imagine what kind of razzing he must have taken? He reports good-naturedly that he also took their tips. Of all the qualities that help during a transition, I've found that the ability to "lighten up" is one of the best. And to realize, like O'Neil did, that this limbo period is not permanent. And someday you, like O'Neil, may have your own "starring" role in life.

Many clients making career transitions must deal with dramatic drops in income. Clients have confided they are living on one-third of the income they used to make. Tim, an abstract painter, is now living on the interest from a small family inheritance—less than he used to pay his secretary. But each day he loves "catching the right light," mixing colors no one has ever mixed and preparing for the Beverly Hills Art show. Will he make it? In Tim's mind he's making it every day—he is living his dream.

Where will you live?

In the '90s, *where* you live need not be driven by career choice, but by *personal* choice. With a plan of action, the right technical equipment, the right capital and lots of ingenuity, you can choose to live in the mountains, in the city, on both coasts or abroad—no matter what profession you want to practice. In fact, you may want to choose where you live before you consider what you want to do.

Just what are the best places in America to live? *Money* magazine publishes its list each summer, comparing about 300 different areas across the country. Another great source is *50 Fabulous Places to Raise Your Family* by Lee and Saralee Rosenberg (Career Press). Check your library for other reference books. According to the U.S. Office of Management and Budget, the best cities for jobs in the 1990s are (in alphabetical order): Atlanta, Boston, Dallas, Houston, Los Angeles, New York, Phoenix, San Diego, San Francisco and Washington D.C.

If you're raising kids, you'll want to choose a family-oriented community. The organization Zero Population Growth—considering 10 factors including population stability, crowding, child health, crime, education, air quality and water resources—came up with these 10 cities as the best places to raise kids (*The Wall Street Journal*, May 26, 1993):

- Burlington, Vt.
- Fargo, N.D. and Moorhead, Minn. (tied)
- Lincoln, Neb.

- Stamford, Conn.
- Champaign-Urbana, Ill.
- Sioux Falls, S.D.
- Salem-Gloucester, Mass.
- Boulder-Longmont, Colo.
- Ann Arbor, Mich.

Zero Population Growth spokesperson, Dianne Sherman says, "We found a strong correlation between the size of a city or metropolitan area and the overall stress on children. Bigger isn't always better."

To find out more about other areas of the country and the job opportunities they offer, check with chambers of commerce, which now send very sophisticated packages and videos about their towns. In fact, some chambers may be ready to "recruit" you to their area if you have a skill they need. Also, most professional organizations have chapters around the country. There are offices for "Forty Plus," the nonprofit job-hunting organization, across the nation. And be sure to check the reference section of the library for the local yellow pages and the National Business Employment Weekly, a newspaper that features job ads throughout the country.

Matching what you want to do with where you want to live can be a creative process. Think about *your* career choice. How could you make it happen in a big city? In a small town? Let's examine these two options with a few different career choices.

1. Want to be a writer/novelist or screenwriter?

Big city: You may choose to be a technical writer at a major computer firm by day and write science fiction by night. You may want to hit New York and open your play off-off Broadway, or come to Hollywood and get a celebrity involved in your project.

Small town: You may turn your family's farm into a writer's retreat and lead some of the short-story workshops yourself. You can modem to your company's headquarters at a Denver cable firm from your ski chalet in Aspen. You can set up a regional repertory theater near Yosemite to test out your screenplays on stage prior to sending them to an agent in L.A.

2. Yearn to be a travel agency owner or tour guide?

Big city: You may choose to lead families on "armchair adventures" by creating multimedia presentations that allow people to experience a "virtual" vacation in their own homes.

Small town: You might offer tours of the dinosaur artifacts in your region or set up a travel agency for the handicapped. You can work via modem and computer with this group who increasingly communicate via TTY or computer bulletin boards.

3. Want to have your own business?

Big city: You may choose to set up your own catering business for VIP events

Small town: You may open a restaurant in the park for summer visitors; in winter you may choose to begin to franchise your operation.

4. Want to sail around the world?

Big city: You may invest in new virtual reality arcades that allow you to "sail" from your shopping center, and then take the profits to invest in a sailboat that you and your friends can "timeshare."

Small town: You may want to teach sailing near your family's summer cabin in warm seasons, and work with a sailboat rental company in Australia or Hawaii off season.

To challenge your creativity, consider small-town/big-city options for the following careers:

- Making a contribution to mankind
- Forest ranger
- Lawyer
- Teacher
- Artist
- Gardener/landscape architect

As you consider your lifestyle choices and where you'd like to live, there are other factors that you should weigh:

- **Your family situation.** Do you have a spouse? Children? Are you a single parent? Does an ex-spouse have visitation rights? Are you single looking for a partner? Do you have any family commitments that might keep you in a certain area?

- **Your bank account.** Do you have at least six-month's living expenses to get you started in your new community? Keep in mind that the cost of living varies greatly from region to region. Six month's living expenses for New Your City or Los Angeles might buy you as much as a year and a half in a small Midwestern town.

- **Your hobbies and leisure life.** Can't live without a quiet walk in the country each weekend? Do you thrive on theater and nightlife? Whether it's rock climbing, reading or rodeo-watching, make sure you choose a place that's compatible with your recreational interests.

- **Your social life.** True, you can meet terrific people just about anywhere you go. But your social life may evolve around family activities, cultural events, the singles scene or your favorite pastime. Keep this in mind when selecting where you want to live.

But what if you can't afford to move?

Like too many of my clients, you may feel limited by lack of resources. There *are* ways to beat the bank.

Consider house swapping. If, for example, you want to taste life in another city or country, there are services all over the country and around the world that allow you to swap your house for another—in the mountains or in a tourist location like Florida—for a month or three months or even a year.

Or investigate house-sitting in the city of your choice. If you're handy, the absentee owner may relish your assistance in fixing up the broken porch or mending the roof.

How about going international?

What if you'd like to live overseas? Several of my clients have made the transition from L.A. to Japan, New York to Europe or small town to small island in Micronesia.

Before you move anywhere, consider these options:

1. You may want to take a leave of absence and live there for a month or two before you make the commitment.

2. You may want to go over for six weeks to interview or set up work projects.

3. You may want to work for an American company that has offices or worksites in these locations. You could have a chance to explore the area first on shorter trips before packing your suitcases.

4. You may want to keep a safety net here—sublet your house, sublet your apartment, and keep a nest egg in the hands of a relative.

If you're committed to going international, be sure to do the following:

1. Study the language ahead of time.

2. Visit the consulate of the country of your choice.

3. Talk to people who've lived there. Most communities have international organizations. Or check out the international house at your local college or university for contacts, input and direction.

4. Most countries have trade associations, such as the Australian Trade Commission, which will be glad to meet with you while you're still living in the U.S.

5. Consider a blind ad in the English-speaking newspaper advertising your skills, or at least subscribe to it to see what job offerings are available.

They did it, so can you!

Here are some lifestyle choices my clients, friends and students have made:

1. From maid service owner in Los Angeles to diner operator in a small Northwest town.

2. From high-pressure traveling sales executive to telephone sales J.O.B. and musician at night at a beach resort town.

3. From manufacturing plant manager in the Midwest to handyman at a North Shore hotel in Hawaii.

4. From real estate investor in Texas to dating service owner in Los Angeles.

5. From musician traveling with big celebrity bands to New Age psychic healing adviser in Sedona, Arizona.

6. From astrologer to therapist in a university town in Nebraska.

7. From university administrator to lawyer on Wall Street.

8. From copy editor to environmental analyst in New Mexico.

9. From television anchor to speech therapist in Alaska.

10. From beauty queen to health counselor at a country club in Puerto Rico.

11. From barrio teacher to educational writer in Washington, D.C.

12. From geologist to character actor at a Florida theme park.

13. From lawyer to playwright off-off Broadway.

14. From computer salesman to interactive television producer in San Francisco's multimedia gulch.

15. From soap opera actress to costume designer for regional theater in the Southwest.

What advice do these people offer?

"What you own is not as important as how you feel inside."

—Salesman-turned-musician

"Allow plenty of spare time to do your own thing."
—Banker-turned-kindergarten teacher

"Get a computer. It will change the way you work, the way you communicate and who you meet. Be sure to buy a modem and a laptop if your budget permits."
—Real estate entrepreneur-turned-inner-city teacher

"Do your own thing until your money runs out."
—Stockbroker-turned-old house renovator

"Don't compromise—go for it even if it means making some sacrifices in how you live for awhile."
—Ad executive-turned-film writer

Many of my clients find that they only rediscover their values and their lifestyle choices by taking some time off. Refreshed, renewed and revitalized, they start again.

Sometimes clients come to me after taking an "enforced" time out—because of family illness, an accident that immobilized them or a life-or-death crisis. They're sure they don't want to go back to their old jobs—and many times they don't even have that option. But they're afraid to go for the dream because they've been out of the job market. This is the same challenge many women who have been raising children face when they want to return to the workplace.

I encourage these people to realize that they can live out their dreams. That they do have the *right* to dream. Life is not punishment. It is here to be enjoyed. Go for it. *Get a life!*

"In the long run," said Eleanor Roosevelt, "when we shape our lives, we shape ourselves. The process never ends until we die. And the choices we make are ultimately our own responsibility."

Homework

1. Ask five people what their idea of a dream life-style is. By comparing their answers with yours, you may be able to sort out what is important to you.

2. If you're married or have children, you may want to take a weekend retreat by yourself to sort out what your personal choices are and how your family is influencing your lifestyle.

3. If you live in a big city, take a mini vacation—a day or so into the country. If you live in a rural area, take the train into the city or drive to a new city you've never visited.

10. Your work philosophy

1. Why do you work? (List five reasons.)

_____

_____

_____

_____

_____

2. What if you could never work again? How would you feel? (List three emotions.)

_____

_____

_____

3. What brings the most fun to your life? What activities offer you the most pleasure?

_____

_____

_____

_____

_____

4. What is the most fun you've ever had at work?

_____

_____

_____

5. What would make work fun for you? Name four things— even if they seem unrealistic. (Yes, you can have a robot do the "grunt" work for you!)

_____

_____

_____

_____

---

11. Working at home?

1. How productive are you when working at home?

_____
_____
_____
_____

2. What is your level of computer literacy?

_____
_____
_____
_____

3. How much do you enjoy dealing with people?

_____
_____
_____
_____

4. How detail-oriented are you?

_____
_____
_____

5. Are you a self-starter?

_____
_____
_____

6. Do you have a space to work at home?

_____
_____
_____

7. Will your family respect your work?

_____

_____

_____

_____

8. How could you build in checks and balances so you could work from your home? Make a list of things you would need (computer, modem, fax machine, space to work, administrative assistance).

_____

_____

_____

_____

_____

_____

_____

_____

9. If you worked from your home, what would you miss?

_____

_____

_____

_____

_____

_____

10. How could you compensate for that at home?

_____

_____

_____

_____

The transition: Making the right turn in life

"Once I knew I wanted to be an artist, I had made myself into one. I did not understand that wanting doesn't always lead to action. Many of the women had been raised without the sense that they could mold and shape their own lives, and so, wanting to be an artist (without the ability to realize their wants) was, for some of them an idle fantasy, like wanting to go the moon."

Judy Chicago
Internationally known artist

The power to mold and shape our own lives? For most of my clients, this discovery is awe-inspiring. For others, it is overwhelming.

Moving toward your dream career is a little like learning to drive. You can take the course, read the book and imagine what it's like to drive. But suddenly, you're in the driver's seat and it's a whole different experience.

Maybe you saw the 1991 movie "Grand Canyon." In one scene, the character Mack, played by Kevin Kline, is teaching his son how to drive. They are in the middle of a busy intersection, the youth hesitates and the van nearly gets hit. "The thing is, it's crazy out there, you've got to react really fast," Mack tells Roberto, his son. "Making a left turn in L.A. is one of the hardest things you're going to learn in life."

And I say to you, don't make a left turn with this transition—instead, make the *right* turn in life for you!

Before you head off on the "open road," I suggest that you get all your tools lined up and your "vehicle" in working order. If you were going to drive from Los Angeles to New York, you'd probably benefit by stopping by the automobile club. There, you'd get a guide to the best routes. But before you even received this information, the travel adviser would insist on knowing your final destination.

I have found that career decisions are destination-driven too. If you want to win your personal race, *you must know where you're going*.

You may be one of those people who likes to just get in the car and go for a drive. But if you use this same philosophy in your career or life, you may not like the results. If you don't know where you're going, your chances of getting there are 100 percent. Great odds—if you want to end up "nowhere" in life.

Here are some tools that may help you while you're still making your way to your final destination.

1. The transition notebook. A three-ring binder is excellent for storing not only business leads, but trade journal articles, references, business cards, etc. Everything will fit into one binder. You can use plastic sleeves to hold materials you don't want to damage with punch holes. You can keep your computer disks in this notebook as well as printouts of letters, mailing lists and more.

2. The accomplishments diary. Once you're on the road, it's hard to see where you've been. As the sweat dripped down my neck while I climbed the Great Wall of China, I even lost sight of how many steps I had climbed. You'll want to list what you've done toward your goal each day. List at least 10 accomplishments. Count everything, from making phone calls, to a trip to the library, to setting up an internship program, to writing in your accomplishments diary.

3. Video or audio tapes. Record your own encouragement tapes and your vows that you will make it to your goals. Make an oral contract with yourself that you will follow through on this venture. When you need a pep talk and your personal board of advisers is not around (see Chapter 9), then listen to your own advice—it sounds so much more powerful on tape. You can also use this method for taping pep talks from friends, advisers or from famous people. I also love to walk up to speakers following panel discussions and get them on tape answering my questions.

4. Phone logs. My clients sometimes talk to as many as 75 different people a week during their transition period. Keep a phone log of names, numbers and addresses, along with a note about what advice they've given you or referrals they may have supplied.

5. Contacts, contacts and more contacts. If you're moving from one profession to another, you'll want to meet as many people as you can—through friends and colleagues if possible. Most of my clients follow this method: When a friend asks if they can help you in your career transition, say yes. Then request that they fax you the names of three people to talk to about something specific. For example, if you want to be a doctor, the topic might be medical ethics or family practice medicine.

Ask that the names be faxed to you because then you can put them directly in your notebook. You'll have the spellings and the phone numbers right. This is an intense time for you—do anything you can to make this process easier on yourself.

Do not, I repeat, do *not* say to your callers "I'll call you back later!" These people want to do something now, especially if you've been fired or laid off. They know that you're in the midst of a transition. Give them something they *can* do for you—it's your time to collect. They might be too busy to help you later.

If you are relocating then get referrals as "gifts." When my client Colleen Sawyer, relationship therapist and romance counselor, was relocating from Los Angeles to Northern California, her friends and relatives asked what they could bring to her going-away party. In addition to a casserole or cake, she asked them to bring names of three people who lived in Northern California. Now notice, she didn't ask for names of three people who could help her with her business—just three names. These names are then a real resource! They might have helped her find a house to rent, a car to buy, a good cleaner or bakery, a reputable day-care—even job leads.

Help comes from all levels. A secretary is just as likely to have contacts for you as is a president of a bank. Some people only want to operate on the top levels—this does not work generally, because the VIPs are too busy to take phone calls or they can't guide you through some of the toughest parts of your transition—which may be more "housekeeping" in nature. So fill your "dufflebag" with contacts at all levels. They'll pay off for you.

A sample transition, step by step

Your objective in your transition process is to get as close as possible to your goal, your goal area and your goal dream career, even if it means getting there a step at a time.

Let's say you're like my client Leonardo, owner of a small printing shop, who aspires to be an executive at an advertising agency. You'll want to follow this type of system, which works in making transitions to most other fields too:

1. Get a subscription to a trade magazine in your chosen field of interest—Leonardo subscribed to *Adweek* and *Advertising Age* for the advertising field.

2. Target who you'd like to meet in your chosen field. First, Leonardo listed 10 ad agencies he read about in *Adweek* and then he made a list of names of people who had won prizes, or who'd done the art direction or copywriting for an advertising campaign he admired.

3. Attend a professional seminar in your dream career field. Many professional publications list conferences or conventions, some of which are open to the public. Others are closed but the exhibits area is open.

Leonardo went to an advertising and marketing conference where he attended seminars and programs, some featuring executives from the agencies he was interested in. He approached several of the executives to ask them questions and get cards. He did not say he was job hunting! If pressed, he said he was doing research.

4. Join a professional association in your dream career field. Do whatever you need to do to get into the association. Most of the time, you can call and say you've just moved to this city and want to join the local branch. The people in charge will probably just send you the materials and you're off and running. Just fill in the application and send your check, and you'll be in the advertising club or the nutritionists association or whatever.

Other times, organizations require candidates to go through a rigorous ordeal reminiscent of "hazing"—several personal recommendations from members in good standing, extensive interviews, etc. Now, if you're transferring professions, getting three recommendations from people you don't know can be tough—not impossible, but tough. Most groups will allow you to go to their meetings as a "guest" of a member at least once. Tactics I've recommended to my clients and used personally include:

- Ask your initial contact at the organization office to invite you.

- Ask the president of the group to invite you.

- Ask the editor or the organization's newsletter to invite you.

- Just show up at the organization's monthly meeting a half-hour early and see if you can attend without an invitation.

Sometimes you can pay the luncheon or dinner fee and just walk in. Once you're in, your goal is not to freeload but to get someone to sponsor you into the group. And if attendees are required to introduce themselves, when it's your turn, don't say you're job hunting. Say that you're new to the area or that you're an independent consultant or freelancer. No one wants to talk to a job hunter.

5. Subscribe to the professional journal of your dream career. For example, when I moved to Hollywood I subscribed to *Emmy Magazine* and *Women in Film* newsletter even before I became a member of these groups, which both require you to be nominated. I got valuable inside information prior to attending any meetings or getting sponsors.

6. Go to a national convention for your chosen field. Want to develop multimedia presentations for corporations on your computer at home, using your new CD ROM drive? Then register for COMDEX, Digital World or Intermedia. Don't know how to find where or what the conferences are all about? Check out the appropriate trade magazines at your library. Call the Los Angeles Convention Center or Javitz Convention Center in New York and ask for the upcoming schedule of conferences. Many conventions let you buy a guest pass for one day or attend the exhibits area for free or a low fee.

7. If you're relocating, subscribe to the local newspaper ahead of time. Most cities will send you the paper for a week—or check your local newsstand and see if the owner can get you the Sunday paper. Most big cities have at least one newsstand with out-of-town papers. In addition, many libraries (especially business libraries) have out-of-town newspapers.

If you want to open a gardening shop in Honolulu, you'll certainly want to subscribe to the *Honolulu Advertiser*, *Pacific Business News* and *Honolulu* magazine. You can begin gathering names, and correspond with the editor or reporters for information.

8. Consider writing an article for a trade magazine to establish yourself—even before you start living your dream career.

My client Susan wanted to get into television—her specialty had been children's clothing. By combining her experience in kids' clothing with an interest in TV, I saw lots of options for her. She took a survey of the top 20 kids' clothing and toy companies to determine what they wanted to see on Saturday morning TV. A magazine called *Electronic Media* (a trade journal for the TV industry) ran her survey in story form. By the time she started to pitch for a top executive position in TV, she was already a published author in the area. It certainly helped get her a $100,000 job!

9. Position yourself as a resource or an expert—not a neophyte. You have years of expertise to offer. All you have to know is how to *translate* your experience. Consider co-authoring a paper with another researcher, or volunteer to help at a group fund-raiser. For example, if you used to operate an advertising specialty firm, you can help with the buttons and badges for the national convention. You can volunteer to serve on the community liaison committee if you've been active in a chamber of commerce in another city—the same principles will apply in your new dream location.

10. Get involved in charity work. One of the easiest ways to get connected in a new city or a new field is to get involved with the favorite charity of your dream field. You'll be able to determine your new industry's favorite charity through newsletters or by asking a chapter executive director. Or you can work with the charity of your choice, look for people in your dream career field and join their committees. Sound too self-serving? Public service is a something-for-something proposition. If it isn't, it will just burn you out.

11. Start a newsletter for your dream career. If you want to own your own photo studio, you may want to start a simple four-page newsletter on your computer. The newsletter might include interviews with experts from photo supply houses or film companies. You may even want to announce a local photo contest. All of this, even before you've got the money for the rent for your photo shop! You'll gain a reputation as the photographer who publishes the *Photo News* and you'll have the advantage of showing off your photos to everyone on your mailing list. You may not even have to pay to print the newsletter—stop by a local printer and offer to trade your photo services for printing.

12. Get stationery and business cards. Yes, even before you start living your dream, you'll need these essentials. "But," you say, "I don't know where my office will be." Use your home address or get a mailing address (not a post office box) from a mailing service—for about $20 a month. You'll also need a phone number that is not answered by your 10-year-old son, your spouse or a "cutesy" phone message. Nothing worse than calling someone for business and getting "Daffy, Suzie, Curt and our dog Spot are out now. Please leave a message." Act professional from the beginning and you'll be treated professionally.

At this point, you're ready to head for the road! Now you'll want to get some experience in your dream career, including:

Internships

Yes, even nonstudents do internships! Many people will take on an intern in this day and age in order to get badly needed help. They may pay minimum wage or expect you to work and learn for free. If you're trained in another area (a CPA who wants to learn photography), you may be able to get training by trading services. If you don't feel comfortable calling this an internship, fine. Consider it real-life research. Whatever you call it, it is an excellent way to get a real taste of day-to-day life in your dream career. Don't wait until you've enrolled in college, graduate school or vocational school to see if you like the new field well enough to pursue it.

Be prepared to be offered a job during your internship. I was, and I turned it down to finish graduate school. What choice would I make—if I had to do it over? I would have worked the job part-time and switched graduate school to part-time. There is always a solution. In this job market you don't want to walk away from dream career opportunities with great people. You can always work out something, even if it means commuting by modem to school or work.

Apprenticeships

Scores of unions, groups and organizations offer apprenticeships. Contact the Bureau of Apprenticeship and Training at the U.S. Department of Labor, 200 Constitution Ave., N.W., Washington, D.C. 20210, or phone 1-202-535-0545. You may be able to set up your own apprenticeship. I've had apprentices in the advertising agency business, in my college administration work and in my own business.

Most of the time these apprenticeships are for people who want to learn for a set period of time—one or three months. And there may be a stipend attached—$500 for three months, for example. Most employers feel more comfortable offering you a stipend than having you work for free. The money can be in one lump sum, paid along the way to cover your gas/lunch expenses, or deferred. (If you accept deferred, you'll probably never see the money—but you can chalk it off if you get a great reference or referrals).

Some of my clients have apprenticed on weekends or nights or early in mornings. Most small to mid-sized firms more readily accept interns or apprentices than do large corporations, which may have stringent rules about "independent contractors."

Part-time work

Many of my clients start out in their dream careers by working part-time. Ava began working at a travel agency, trading her bookkeeping skills to learn the Sabre computer system. I've had other clients trade for training programs or for on-the-job experience.

What if you're employed full-time, or don't have time for an internship or apprenticeship? Then consider a *day or week on the job*. It is much more effective than the traditional R&R (reference and referral) interviews. One of my clients, a high-powered lawyer, tried this approach. By "shadowing" one of his clients in the hotel field, he was able to get an idea of what it would take to set up a reservation system for his dream of opening a small resort in the Northwest.

24-hour immersion

If you have no time for an apprenticeship, yet you'd like something more organized or thorough than the rather informal "day on the job," you'll want to do a 24-hour immersion. It's kind of like taking a crash course in a foreign language—except you're prepared, you're *living* your dream for a day, and you're meeting valuable contacts. The 24-hour immersion will include:

1. Eight hours of preparation. This is broken down as follows:

- Two hours of reading about your chosen career in trade journals.
- Two hours of reading about the company where you'll do your 24-hour immersion. Get hold of its annual report, corporate brochures, employee newsletters, etc.
- Two hours of listing which topics or issues about the business you're pursuing.
- Two hours of listing key names and researching information about them. You wouldn't want to do

an immersion in the advertising field without knowing who the top 20 ad agencies are. Most industry leaders write books or have articles written about them. You should be able to quote them during your 24-hour immersion.

2. Eight hours on the job. Schedule a day on the job. Use your networking contacts or contacts from a professional organization to get in the door of the company or field you're interested in.

If you have difficulty getting someone to allow you to spend a full day in the offices, you may want to patch together an eight-hour day by visiting three offices. But be sure to talk to people in the areas you're interested in. For example, don't leave an ad agency until you've talked to a copywriter—or two or three—if that is an area you'd like to pursue.

Never talk about a *job*. Now, if someone starts asking *you* about a job, immediately arrange for a lunch or a cup of coffee later in the week. Follow up the next day with a fax confirming when and where you'll meet them. Who knows? It just may lead to the big break you've dream of.

3. The evaluation. Take two hours to recap your experience, translating notes or transcribing tape recordings you may have made on the job. Then spend a couple hours adding your input. Follow this with two hours of discussion with people in your chosen field—maybe even the same people you "worked" with on the job.

What to do after the 24-hour immersion? That depends on your experiences and your response. You may decide to:

1. Go back to school in your chosen profession.
2. Change dream careers.

3. Pursue an internship or apprenticeship.

4. Move to another city to pursue career opportunities there.

5. Add to your network the people you did your immersion with.

6. Add to your personal board of advisers some of the contacts you made during your immersion.

7. Be prepared for opportunities by creating a one-page biography that summarizes your strengths and achievements.

8. Develop a functional resume listing your accomplishments by category, rather than listing your job experience chronologically. The functional resume will make it easier for a prospective employer to identify your transferable skills.

Your goal is to enter your dream career from a position of power, not as a beggar. You have work experience to share. You have insights. You have talents and contacts that will translate into dollars for your potential employer or customers buying your products or services.

Your "competitive edges" on your trip to your dream career are:

- Your experiences
- Your contacts
- Your credentials
- Your abilities/skills
- Your opinions
- Your business savvy
- Your street smarts

The tools and methods given in this chapter to help boost you along the road toward your dream career are not just innovative, they have been proven successful time and again. They will speed up your transition time. They will put you back into the driver's seat. You can't control the job market, but you can package yourself for success.

Designing your dream career map

What if your dream starts to overwhelm you? What if your emotions start to scare even you? What if you can't possibly see how you will get from here to there? Stay on course by designing a map that will guide you toward your dream career.

Here's how Rebecca's career map looked:

Now: new car salesperson at the local Toyota dealership.

Goal: professional race car driver.

Route:

Step 1. Rent every race car movie there is. (More enjoyable to Rebecca, who hates to read.)

Step 2. Subscribe to racing magazines to keep on desk at work. (Not even to read, necessarily, but just to remind her that her dream is near all of the time.)

Step 3. Open a savings account for dream career. (Her income is unpredictable so the money is set aside to help her.)

Step 4. Make plans to go to a major sportscar race. (Indianapolis 500 or Daytona. She can use her contacts to get behind-the-scene passes.)

Step 5. Get photos with race cars. (Perhaps even sitting in a race car at the Speedway so she can use that as a visual reminder of where she is going.)

Step 6. Get autographs or pictures with one of the female racers.

Step 7. Write to a woman racer for encouragement. Check the local library or sports department of the local paper for background on women racers.

Step 8. Talk to a reporter at a newspaper or magazine that covers racing—find out what it takes to get your own race car sponsored.

Step 9. Take a race car class. (Rebecca may even meet an executive from a company that could sponsor her own car when she's ready.)

Your personalized dream career map provides a sense of peace along the way. Kind of like looking at the mountain top as you climb. If it becomes hidden by the haze and the smog, then you may lose interest or give up along the way up.

As Anne Morrow Lindbergh said, "It isn't for the moment that you are struck that you need courage, but for the long uphill climb back to sanity and faith and security."

Homework

1. Create your dream career map, identifying where you are now, where you plan to go, and the steps you intend to take to get there. Develop a chart or graph on your computer, create a game board—or just list the steps on a piece of paper. However you do it, keep it handy so you can plot your progress as you go along.
2. Make an outline for your biography. If you need help writing one, ask a friend or former colleague

to help you draft a biography that highlights your achievements.

3. Purchase or check out a good book on resumes from the library and begin to develop a list of your "transferable skills" and achievements.

4. Make a list of associations or organizations for your dream career.

5. Call or write two or three professional groups and ask for their "general information packets." Many have brochures that feature up-to-date opportunities in the fields.

6. Subscribe to at least one professional journal in your chosen field. Or call your local or university library to see if they stock the publication.

7. Start gathering background information on VIPs in your chosen field. These people can become your role models (see Chapter 8 for more details) or personal advisers, if not job contacts.

12. Your dream career: Capitalize on trends

Write down your dream career idea inspired by the following trends:

1. The rise of the Pacific Rim: _____
_____
_____
_____
_____

2. The '90s is the decade of women in leadership: _____
_____
_____
_____
_____

3. The age of biology: _____
_____
_____
_____

4. Religious revival: _____
_____
_____
_____
_____

5. Triumph of the individual: _____
_____
_____
_____
_____

13. Living the dream now

Your goal is to begin to live your dream career even before you make the final transition. What ways can you start that now?

1. If you want to relocate, how can you find out more about that area of the country/world?

_____

_____

_____

_____

2. Find out what trade shows are coming to your area. Jot down the names of the shows here.

_____

_____

3. How could attending any of these shows help you in your dream career?

_____

_____

_____

4. What journals can you subscribe to for your dream career? Does your local library have them?

_____

_____

_____

5. What volunteer work could you do to gain some experience in your dream career?

_____

_____

_____

Role models:
They did it,
so can you!

To make this career transition a smooth one, surround yourself with the *right people*. Positive, supportive people who believe in your dream, too. But, in addition, it's important that you get in touch with individuals that you can emulate. People who can teach you something, give you advice, guide you with the wisdom of their own experience, inspire you to become as successful as they have.

In other words, find yourself some role models. When you're soaking in perspiration, you need inspiration.

How important is it to have a role model? Even those we might consider choosing as role models for ourselves, we discover, often have role models of their own. For Hillary Rodham Clinton, imaginary conversations with her role model Eleanor Roosevelt provide a sense of direction before public talks. Hillary says she actually speaks—sometimes aloud—to Eleanor, seeking guidance and opinions.

One individual who might serve as a role model for anyone who's suffered great tragedy and aspires to turn grief into a positive direction is my client Candy Lightner. Candy's daughter was killed by a drunk driver. As a result of this tragedy, she transitioned from a successful real

estate salesperson to an extremely well-known political activist in a matter of days. Her experiences in the creation of
Mothers Against Drunk Driving (MADD) have helped me to
identify some of the traits of successful dream career makers.

1. They can feel, visualize and describe their new
   career in detail even before they live it.
2. They had a life-changing experience that encouraged them or discouraged them regarding their
   dream career (if they were discouraged, they found a
   way to overcome it at this time).
3. They are relentless—nothing will stop them.
4. They are driven by *yearning*, not earning.
5. They know they made the right choice—they brag
   about it the way some people brag about their
   kids or their prize petunias.
6. They are confident about their future.
7. They see this new career not as the culmination
   but as a bridge to their future.
8. They know they were "meant to do this."
9. They are missionaries—they talk about the dream,
   they teach the dream, they live the dream.
10. They know failure is only split-seconds away from
    success, as any Olympic athlete will remind you.
11. They have support, and they support themselves.
12. When the going gets rough, they turn to people
    who help invigorate their own inner resources.

What? You don't have a role model? Haven't discovered
anyone in the catering/landscaping/massage therapy field that
you can turn to for inspiration? Don't despair. It's not that
difficult to identify a valuable role model, and you don't

necessarily have to turn to your specific field to find one. Here are some exercises that may help you:

1. Reacquaint yourself with childhood heroes. Many dream career makers know they have a date with destiny even as a child. And it is while growing up that they usually find their first influential role models.

As children, we all have heroes. I encourage all of my clients to rediscover their favorite childhood books and heroes and heroines. My favorite kids' book, *Susan and the Rain* is about a little girl who is afraid of rain until her grandparents send her a raincoat with boots and umbrella to match. Then she ventures out to splash in the puddles with glee for the very first time. The sun comes out and a rainbow forms and all is well. As silly as it sounds, I often pretend I have an imaginary raincoat that shields me from life's rain of disappointments when the going gets rough. The analogy never fails to prompt a chuckle.

Whether you turned to a literary character such as Huck Finn or Scarlett O'Hara, or an enigmatic celebrity—whether John Wayne or James Dean—for inspiration, examine your feelings about that hero and determine whether this character exhibits the traits you feel are valuable today to achieve your new dream career.

2. Don't forget real-life heroes. How about Mrs. Piper, your third-grade teacher, who encouraged you toward a career in writing after you won the class haiku contest? Or Coach Stout, who, despite the fact that you struck out every time you were up to bat, always reminded you that you were the fastest runner on the Little League team? Don't overlook teachers, coaches or dance instructors—even grandparents or parents— who may have had the qualities for a good role model.

3. Consider historical figures. One of my role models is Abraham Lincoln. To determine why I've really admired him throughout my life, I did some research and found out he was a brooder, he outwitted clever politicians at their own game and he educated himself by studying *Aesop's Fables*, the poetry of Robert Burns and the tragedies of Shakespeare.

Actually, I was pleased to learn that Lincoln and I had shared some things. When we're attracted to a particular historical character, it may be that their traits and personalities are more important to us than their actual contribution or experiences. Thus, an actor can find inspiration from a general. An architect can be guided by a coach. And a communications professional, like myself, can find direction from a Civil War president!

4. Examine a favorite celebrity. C'mon, admit it. Even if we don't aspire to become an actor, musician or per-former of some sort, most of us can identify at least one celebrity we've fantasized about being—or being *like*. Whether it's Elvis or Mick Jagger, Madonna or Marilyn Monroe, these charismatic individuals often exhibit some valuable traits that signal success. And we should examine our screen heroes and heroines for these characteristics.

5. Don't forget *real* people. Your former bosses, co-workers, associates, clients or even friends. Sure, they're not famous—yet. But maybe your first supervisor who, with determination and decency, broke through the glass ceiling to become the first female executive vice president in the company, provided a few good early lessons on what it takes to succeed. Or your best friend who left the insurance agency two years ago to build his own business as a fishing guide may be able to walk you through some of your own fears about change.

Some of my clients choose real people as role models and they turn to these mentors not only to inspire them but to confide in them. (I refer more specifically to these people as your personal board of advisers—see Chapter 9 for more details).

Now that I've given you some suggestions on where to find your role models, consider these points of advice as well:

1. Pick someone intuitively, based on your interest in their achievements and sense of values, not just their reputation, personality or credentials.

2. Pick someone who has traits that you don't have but would love to acquire.

3. Don't worry about what other people think of your role models. I admire Jane Fonda. A career counselor once tried to talk me out of considering her a role model because of her political stands. Role models are human, they make their own choices, they have their own problems—you get to admire the best in them!

4. Choose more than one role model. My role models include Lincoln, Jane Fonda, Tom Peters and my second-grade teacher. Each inspires me for a different reason.

5. Keep a file on your role models. Or toss stories of people you admire into a covered box—you know, the kind used for valentine exchanges at school, with the slot on the top. Make the slot large enough for your hand. And when the going gets rough, stick your hand in and pull out a "role model reminder"—a quote or a case history or something else that may inspire you.

The trouble with role models is that they are not there at 3 a.m. when you're dealing with the books that don't balance or a mortgage you can't afford to pay this month. That's when I've found my role model box—as well as books, audio tapes and videotapes of motivational speakers, leaders and fictional and historical heroines—invaluable.

Getting through tough times

Most books, magazine articles, television shows and movies make it look so easy to reach your goals. Even the tear jerkers show champions who face obstacles, then dramatically break through. Yet in working with thousands of corporate role models, I've found they all have their doubts, they all have their ups and downs, they are all scared at some time. They cry, they scream, they miss appointments.

But it's not the vulnerability that gets them into *People* magazine or on "Entertainment Tonight" and "Lifestyles of the Rich and Famous." It's not their fear or failure that makes them so appealing to Donahue, Oprah or Geraldo. No, it is their triumph.

In the midst of your transition, you, too, may face challenges. You may run out of money, you may feel inadequate. You may feel like stopping five feet from your goal. Anthony Robbins, in his fascinating book *Awaken the Giant Within*, says that many people do this.

But by having a role model to turn to, you may feel inspired, not tired. And you may find their failures more inspiring than their success stories. Not all stars are overnight celebrities as you can see by the following examples:

- **Lauren Bacall** was once a theater usher. She probably got gum on her shoes and was hollered at by rowdy patrons.
- **Carol Burnett** was a hatcheck girl. It sounds more like the premise for one of her TV skits—I'll bet she did use this later for a comedy sketch.

- **Sean Connery** delivered milk in England. (See Chapter 1 for more about his pre-acting experiences.)

- Next time you're in a shoe store, you may look at the salesperson with new respect when you find out that **Bill Cosby** also sold shoes along his path to success.

- **Barbara Walters** can probably identify with her sponsors for her TV specials, because she once worked as a secretary for an advertising agency.

- **Fred Astaire** was once told he couldn't dance, and **Paul Newman** was told he couldn't act when he first started out.

- It's said that **Sir Laurence Olivier** tripped over scenery and fell into the footlights, prompting laughter from the audience and cast on his stage debut.

Knowing that other successful individuals have faced failure and setbacks may give you some hope in times of stress and despair. But this is also time to turn to one of the best role models you'll ever have—*you*.

Yes, don't underestimate the power of *you*. You've probably faced other problems and solved them, overcome them or survived them in the past.

I keep a photo of myself atop the Great Wall of China on my bedroom wall. I believe that if I can get myself from the Ohio housing project where I was raised to Beijing and to the top of the Great Wall, I can do anything. Sometimes, just looking at the picture is enough to inspire me.

You may find that a photo of you in a triumphant moment—climbing a mountain, speaking to a crowd, at graduation, on your wedding day or your child's first birthday may be enough to inspire you back on the track of positive thinking.

Many of my clients become their own best role models when they "teach their dream." Indeed, sharing the dream may help *them* realize it, too. My client Louise Levison, entrepreneurial consultant, teaches a course called "Bridging the Gap"—providing valuable business skills to filmmakers at the UCLA extension entertainment studies program. Levison has parlayed her course content into an upcoming book for film entrepreneurs who want to create their own businesses.

Another client, Jim Pasternak, who wrote the movie "Cousins," has become a master coach for directors doing their first major films. In addition, he teaches a 16-week workshop on directing.

Sometimes teaching can even *launch* a dream career. Sarah came to me because she wanted to be a film critic. She was a successful high school principal but film was her real love. She'd taken some courses in film review-writing and had submitted some film reviews, but so far no breaks.

I encouraged her to start her own film review society in her local suburb of Los Angeles. Today, she not only heads that group, which has grown to 500 members, but has encouraged major sponsors to help launch her first regional film festival next summer.

By teaching and sharing her love of film she has created a business. And by doing so she has become her own best role model. Now her witty film reviews are read by a guaranteed audience of 500 influential VIPs who attend her society seminars and workshops.

Your role models may be perfect additions to your personal board of advisers. As your "cheerleaders" and guides in this new game of work, they are your air traffic controllers to reaching the stars. See the next chapter for how you can recruit a championship team for your championship season in life.

Homework

1. Gather your inspirational poems, stories, letters into one box or folder. Keep it where you can find it at 3 a.m.

2. Buy or check out an inspirational book or video-tape each week while you are reading this book or setting up your "master plan" for your career transition.

3. Call or write someone you admire today to tell them how he or she has inspired you. Mail the letter and don't expect a return reply—if you get one that's a bonus.

4. Answer the following questions:

   a. Is there a famous person, historical figure or celebrity you admire? Who is it and why?

   b. What was your favorite childhood book? Is there a heroine or hero or analogy (like "The Little Engine That Could") that can inspire you along your path?

   c. What do you have in common with your role model? What skills or talents does your role model have that you'd like to acquire? How are your backgrounds different?

   d. What three things have you learned about living your dream from your role model?

   e. Do you have a photo that shows you in a moment of triumph? A trophy or badge that demonstrates a past success?

14. It's not just what you know, it's *who* you know

1. List individuals you know who might be able to offer financial support to enable you to achieve your goal. (No, you don't have to ask for money, but put their names down anyway).

_____   _____
_____   _____
_____   _____

2. List any individuals you know who are celebrities or who have celebrity contacts.

_____   _____
_____   _____
_____   _____

3. List individuals you know who are well-connected in your dream field.

_____   _____
_____   _____
_____   _____

4. Who do you know in various parts of the country? (You may have many names, put down the first that come to mind now).

West:_____   Midwest:_____
_____   _____
_____   _____

East: _____   South: _____

_____   _____

_____   _____

5. List anyone—famous or otherwise—who you believe could help you—if they knew you.

_____   _____

_____   _____

_____   _____

_____   _____

6. Who could help you make your dreams come true? Check off the ones you'd like to meet?

☐ investors _____
☐ bankers _____
☐ employer who believes in you _____
☐ business partner(s) _____
☐ personal assistant _____
☐ realtor _____
☐ landlord _____
☐ technician _____
☐ inventor _____
☐ marketing adviser _____
☐ franchise broker _____
☐ talent/literary agent _____
☐ advertising agency _____
☐ business broker _____
☐ fairy godmother _____
☐ graphic artist _____
☐ housekeeper _____
☐ wife/husband/partner _____

15. Who do you admire in history?

1. What historical figure do you wish you had known?

_____

_____

a. What advice do you expect he or she might have given you regarding your dream career?

_____

_____

2. What historical figure do you dislike? Anything that you can learn *not* to do from this person?

_____

_____

3. Is there an inspirational quote from your favorite historical character—or another person—to help you through the tough times or motivate you?

_____

_____

4. If you could have been a famous person in history, who would it have been?

_____

_____

a. What would you have done differently?

_____

_____

If you haven't read a biography of your favorite historical person, check one out from your library today.

16. Who inspired you when you were a kid?

1. List five individuals who inspired you as you grew up.

_____
_____
_____
_____
_____

2. What was your favorite childhood book?

_____
_____

3. Is there any way the book can inspire you in your career transition?

_____
_____

4. What was your favorite TV show?

_____
_____

5. How was the world of "work" portrayed on that show?

_____
_____
_____

6. How would you change it to fit your new role in life? Go ahead, rewrite the show. Use extra paper if you need it.

_____
_____
_____
_____

17. How can your role models help you?

1. Which celebrities (politicians, movie stars, athletes) do you admire today?

_____

_____

_____

_____

_____

_____

_____

a. Why do you admire them?

_____

_____

_____

_____

_____

_____

_____

_____

b. What is the one trait you admire and covet most?

_____

_____

_____

_____

_____

_____

_____

c. How do you differ from them? Good or bad?

_____
_____
_____
_____
_____
_____
_____

2. Who do you admire in your community?

_____
_____
_____
_____
_____
_____
_____

3. Do you "talk" to your role models? If you do, what are your conversations like?

_____
_____
_____
_____
_____
_____

4. If you could have a hologram of a famous person near your desk, how could they help you with your work?

_____
_____
_____
_____
_____

Building your support system: Your family of choice

> *"I start with the premise that the function of leadership is to produce more leaders, not more followers."*
>
> Ralph Nader

Along the road to your next career, your family of *chance*—your spouse, children and parents—may lose interest in your ongoing adventure. To them, it might be a little like watching slides of someone else's vacation. They aren't part of it and they may think you are foolish for going to the beach instead of the mountains.

Even the most supportive family may start fraying around the edges if the bills don't get paid on time or when you're going to school three nights a week to earn a law degree at age 54 and could be retiring early like the guy next door...*if* you would have stayed at the bank.

That's why you need to create your *family of choice*—not chance, as discussed in Chapter 2. This new family may provide all of the support that your family of chance can't, won't or doesn't know how to provide. Even if your family and friends stand the test of time and support your dream career choices, you'll want to design a support system with the care that NASA puts into the team that launches its spaceships.

It's up to you to set up your personal board of advisers. Otherwise, you'll find that flying solo to your dream is a little like navigating a 747 without a flight crew or ground crew. Some of my clients actually create a formal board, others just keep a resource list of VIPs. Other clients meet with their advisers collectively every three months or so; some touch base just once a year. And many choose to meet with a personal adviser once a week to spur them on to success. Some make it a policy not to *pay* their board, others believe that a fair exchange is important and pay them an hourly rate they can afford. Sometimes a home-made dinner or a box of cookies is enough. Other times, actual preferred stock in a business is offered to even out the financial exchange.

British film director Michael Winner has said somewhat facetiously that "a team effort is a lot of people doing what I say." Well, your team effort to launch your dream career is a lot of people saying what you're doing is *terrific*, then being there when you need specific input, ideas or resources.

Quite frankly, you don't necessarily want total boldfaced honesty at this point in your new career. Dream careers start off like small infants, a step at a time. Imagine a parent saying to a small child starting to walk, "Come on, put down your toe first, not your heel. Arch your back. Anatomically you're out of line. Straighten your knees, pace your steps." The kid would never take a step, let alone cross the room.

At this point in pursuing success in your dream career, you need cheerleaders and coaches. You need loving outstretched arms and slaps on the back and applause.

Sound too "Pollyanna-ish?" Then think of watching a tennis match or a golf competition. If the players could hear the sports commentators live they would probably crumble into little balls on the spot. The great coaches are catalysts, not critics.

In forming your family of choice, you'll want to start with the cheerleaders. Just like the Raiders and the Dallas Cowboys have tryouts, you can set aside a week or two for recruiting your squad.

Your group of supporters will come from a number of sources:

1. People who know you

- relatives
- spouses or partners
- neighbors
- clergy
- employees
- colleagues
- golf/tennis pals
- bosses
- association members
- friends

The good news is that these people know you and your abilities. The bad news is that some may see you only in your old role of bank manager or school principal or aerospace engineer or as Johnny's Little League coach. They see the caterpillar, not the butterfly about to emerge. They may also be jealous or competitive about your ambition. They may be hurt that you don't want to stay as "one of the guys or gals" but you'd prefer to "go it alone." So be sure you select your advisers from those individuals who have the flexibility to see your potential.

2. People who *knew* you

You may have lost touch with some individuals who've worked closely with you, who've been supportive of you in other endeavors and who'd be happy to offer you the advice and guidance you may need now. (This is one reason why it's important to maintain your network.) Now's the time to get back on the phone! Chances are these people will be more than happy to become part of your life once again.

- former bosses
- past employees
- former co-workers
- suppliers
- classmates
- college professors
- counselors
- members of volunteer groups
- seminar leaders
- news reporters

Although you may not have been in touch with these people for awhile, many of them may remember you positively. You may even have inspired them to move forward. Compared to your family and friends and colleagues of today, contacts from the past may *expect* you to have changed. They may not be the least bit surprised that you are changing again. Time provides a sense of perspective for many people.

3. People you'd like to know

There are probably a lot of people you'd like to get to know, whether they're world-famous celebrities or perhaps just locally known, or whether they're friends of friends you've heard about.

Your colleague may have told you about his terrific lawyer who always seems to have time for him. A friend who just started her own catering business may have raved about the terrific job her PR person did in launching the company in the media. You may have read about someone in a trade magazine. Your parents may know the owner of the bank. Your neighbors may be related to a venture capitalist or a real estate mogul who owns the land you'd like for your new summer resort.

4. The people you meet by "accident"

Keep your antenna up as you go about your day-to-day business. You never know when you might run into someone who could be a good candidate for your personal board of advisers. Talk to people—the guy at the bus stop (could be president of his own small start up), the woman waiting in the dentist office (her accounting experience may just be what you were looking for), the man sitting next to you on the plane (he may be returning from checking out a company for investment purposes).

My clients tell me once they make the list of people they want to meet, the "matches" start to happen. In fact, one producer met Steven Spielberg's mother at the dentist, a comedy writer met Carol Burnett's assistant at the deli, Arnold Schwarzenegger was in front of a make-up artist in the supermarket line, Sly Stallone's security adviser consulted on an alarm system for my client, a business manager. Some of these students and clients took advantage of the situation and turned it into a golden opportunity; others felt awkward and shy and let the moment pass.

A real winner is an actor client of mine whose real name is *Eastwood*. "Clint" got a telephone call on his machine one day—obviously a wrong number. They wanted to talk about the new picture they wanted *him* to star in. My client returned the call from his message machine and turned it into an audition. No, not for the lead but for a secondary role.

As you develop your family of choice, think of the different areas where you'll need assistance. For example, you may feel inadequately equipped to handle any number of financial issues—such as:

- bank loans
- financial plans
- mortgage
- business plans
- refinancing
- prospectus

- lease
- tax assistance
- accounting

- letters of credit
- credit

Then, think of the types of professionals you might want to tap for their expertise. You might turn to the following for help:

- bankers
- venture capitalists
- creditors
- suppliers
- real estate brokers

- business strategists
- financial planners
- accountants
- investors

Don't forget your emotional needs. In addition to financial, marketing, sales, research and other areas, you need to consider individuals who can give you the ongoing emotional support you'll need. Consider individuals who can offer:

- counseling
- constructive criticism
- support
- input
- guidance

- "just a kind ear"
- direction
- encouragement
- conversation
- perspective

Resources for contacts

Consider the following resources. They have helped me during four major relocations to different cities—New York, San Francisco, Honolulu and Los Angeles.

- referral organizations (Some provide free services. SBA-sponsored SCORE is a group of retired professionals who can offer business assistance.)

- alumni groups
- local high school/college job bureaus
- chambers of commerce
- Forty-Plus
- Retired Senior Volunteer Group
- part-time and nonprofit employment bureaus (In Los Angeles, there's a group called "The Job Factory," which provides part-time assistance.)
- professional organizations
- 800 referral numbers (1-800-LAWYER, etc.)
- church/synagogue contacts
- mechanics/dentists/dry cleaners/lawyers (All have a broad base of clients and can frequently refer you to qualified professionals.)
- ads in local papers—even fliers posted may bring you support.

Forming your board of advisers

After completing the worksheet on page 161, where you've identified candidates for your family of choice, pare down the list to your top candidates and gather phone numbers and addresses for them.

Before you contact these individuals to ask them the serve on your board, prepare a thorough action plan or brochure that indicates how your new career will be successful. Have professional stationery designed for your dream career (or at least a rough draft of it if you want to get a graphic artist on your board).

Then you need to approach each contact for a meeting. The manner in which you approach these individuals will vary, depending upon your relationship with them. Of course, it's a snap with friends, acquaintances and business associates. But what about those you don't know? Celebrities and leaders in your community or field?

Approach this situation much as you would trying to land a job interview with someone you don't know. First, you want to find someone who knows this individual. Never underestimate the power of a *name* to open the right doors! The best situation would be to have a personal introduction. If this is out of the question, ask your friend to make a call to the individual before you contact him or her, giving you a positive referral.

If you can't dig up any personal connection to the individual you want to contact, your best bet is to send an attention-getting mailing. Include a well-written letter as well as any helpful material that will enhance your credibility—a press release announcing your new venture or clippings about you in the local paper. Then, after mailing the package, follow up in a week with a phone call and ask for a meeting.

One of my clients got his new business prospective into the hands of a potential investor he couldn't get through to after numerous phone calls.

How did he do it? He stopped by the investor's office during lunch hour. The secretary wasn't there. He walked down the hall and put the prospectus on the top of the guy's desk with a post-it note that said "MUST SEE!" By 3 p.m., the investor had called him and set up a meeting for the next morning. In three weeks he had his money.

Many of my clients have contacted hard-to-approach VIPs by volunteering on a community board, or helping out at a fund-raising event that they're involved in.

Others have hung out at the country club or golf course. One even offered to caddie for the executive and then had a captive audience. Sound fantastic? Time after time, my clients tell me these extraordinary actions are needed to get extraordinary results. Your dream career shouldn't be ordinary; why should your approaches to making it happen be?

Choose your advisers wisely, for they are your family of believers—your "apostles," your gurus and your cabinet officers.

Just as you are often your best role model, you may also be your best adviser, too. The buck must stop with you. Don't be swayed by anyone if you truly believe you are right. John Malone, the head of TCI (Telecommunications Inc.), the big cable company, had to threaten to shut down his firm several times in the early stages when his creditors and advisers pressured him too tightly. He knew he would triumph if given the latitude to do so.

After all, you're not living your dream career as you did a job in the past. You're living your dream for *you*.

Homework

1. Look for referral services in your community for lawyers, accountants, therapists, etc.
2. Ask friends for recommendations for "openings" on your board. Be judicious in your choices. Don't be influenced by "volunteers" you don't feel comfortable with—no matter how famous they are.
3. Clip newspaper articles and magazine interviews with VIPs you'd like to have on your board.
4. Start interviewing for your board members now. Do at least one interview weekly until you have five to six people who have agreed to "work" for you.
5. Meet your political leaders. Meet your senator, your congressman/woman and even someone from the mayor's office. Even if you're not political, these people are great resources.

---

18. Contacts for help with day-to-day problems

Where could you find assistance if you need to handle a domestic or work emergency as you're going through your career transition? Do a little research now and have these vital contacts ready, so you can handle any unexpected situation successfully.

Childcare assistance. (What if you have to go out of town at the last minute?)

Babysitter/Childcare service_____

_____

_____

Babysitter/Childcare service_____

_____

Babysitter/Childcare service_____

_____

_____

Car care. (Car breaks down right before an important interview.)

Auto mechanic_____

_____

_____

Car rental_____

_____

_____

Car rental_____

_____

_____

Housekeeping. (What with your classes, J.O.B. and apprenticeship, you don't have time to clean before your mother-in-law arrives in two days.)

Cleaning service_____

Cleaning service_____

Cleaning service_____

Health. (You don't have time to let that cold turn into bronchitis.)

Doctor_____

Doctor_____

24-hour health clinic_____

Office help. (You just got a great freelance project dumped in your lap...with less than a one-week turnaround!)

Part-time help_____

Temporary agency_____

Consultant_____

Computer assistance. (Whether you use your computer for work only, or all your bills, budget and personal information is stored in that hard drive, you can't afford a computer crash at any time.)

Computer consultant_____

---

19. Creating your family of choice

1. List the people you know who are supportive of you (relatives, friends, employees, colleagues, bosses, neighbors).

_____   _____
_____   _____
_____   _____
_____   _____

2. List people you've known in the past who might be helpful—yes, even if you haven't been in touch for awhile (bosses, employees, suppliers).

_____   _____
_____   _____
_____   _____
_____   _____

3. List the people you'd _like_ to know (government officials, celebrities, VIPs, corporate executives).

_____   _____
_____   _____
_____   _____
_____   _____

4. How have you met the people who've been influential in your life? (Personal introduction? On an airplane?)

_____   _____
_____   _____
_____   _____
_____   _____

20. Who can you put on your board of advisers?

1. Accountant _____
2. Lawyer _____
3. Politician _____
4. Expert in field _____
5. Mentor _____
6. Supplier _____
7. Spiritual adviser _____
8. Emotional adviser _____
9. Role model _____
10. Celebrity _____
11. Research person _____
12. Magazine/newspaper editor _____
13. Graphic artist _____
14. PR person/Advertising agency owner _____
15. Computer expert _____
16. Others _____

_____

_____

_____

_____

_____

Am I doing the right thing? 20 Qs and As

> *"Once success starts, it can never stop. For success is never ending. Even the setting of the sun does not mark an end to the day that is past, for that day is given eternal life as it becomes a part of irrevocable history!"*
>
> Dr. Robert H. Schuller
> *Success is Never Ending, Failure is Never Final*

I remember the time I was relocating to Hawaii to work as a vice president at the largest advertising agency there. It was a very exciting and scary time in my life. I'd just filed for divorce two days before. My whole world was changing. The moving men were in the kitchen packing the glasses and dinnerware and I kidded with them that maybe I wouldn't go after all. They said, "Well, your stuff's going anyway, we're working for your new boss, not you." It was at that moment that I truly discovered the power of the *fait accompli*, a French phrase I interpret as "It's happening. You either go with the flow or get pulled in by the undertow." In other words, "It's out of your hands, baby!" Sure, I could have stopped everything, but I wanted to go. I was just having my own version of stage fright. For some celebrities, stage fright is a motivator—it excites them. For other clients, I've seen it devastate and debilitate them so badly, they just can't function.

As you move along your path to success and your dream career, you may experience frustration, difficulties and setbacks. In his book, Dr. Robert Schuller says this is one of the parts of realizing your dream. He explains, "My testimony is that there must be a last-minute test and trial before the great triumphant moment of stunning success. I have always experienced pain, suffering or costly difficulties at this stage." Schuller says it was in one of those times he wrote a most inspirational passage:

> *"When you think you have exhausted all possibilities, remember this: You haven't."*

What comes next? According to Dr. Schuller, it's the "dream-come-true."

But along the way to the fulfillment, you, too, will probably have plenty of questions. And that's when you'll want to turn to the "Ghostbusters." No, not Bill Murray and Dan Ackroyd from the movie of the same name, but your own crew of personal advisers, role models, inspirational leaders and, of course, your own inner strength and spirituality.

Keep this book handy, though, and you'll be able to refer to what I have found are 20 of the most frequently asked questions about how to make your next career your dream career:

1. What if I don't know what I want to do?

My experience in helping more than 2,000 people create their dream careers is that most people *do* have some idea of what they'd like to do. Many times, fear, economics and doubt cloud the true goals.

I suggest that you take the time necessary to identify your true interests. You may want to set aside a few hours, a few days or even longer to narrow these down. Be sure to fill out the worksheets in this book, including "Your skills, your career" on page 63, and "Your work philosophy" on page 113.

Further exploration of these interests could include college extension courses, internships, apprenticeships, interviews with individuals in the fields you're interested in, or even some 24-hour immersions (see Chapter 7).

Remember, you may have as many as seven careers in your lifetime. So those of you who are torn between two or three different career options may actually be able to do them all in some manner. For example, if you like real estate but want to teach, you may be able to conduct your own seminars on real estate. If you want to sail the high seas, you may be able to do so by investing in a charter sailboat with a group of friends and take turns "captaining" the ship throughout the year.

Having a career in the '90s does not mean having a 9-to-5 job. It does not necessarily mean doing *just one thing*. As more and more jobs become entrepreneurial in nature, so will our workstyles. Income may come from a number of different profit centers. In order to make your goal of $50,000 per year, you may want to combine the incomes from the charter sailboat business with your real estate seminars, with your investment income and with a part-time J.O.B. working for a real estate firm three days a week.

2. What's the difference between a dream career and a J.O.B.?

It might be easier to understand if you look at it this way:

J Just
O Only a
B Bridge

You're on the job—you're doing someone *else's* business. Your goal is to make this job a bridge to your new career. Enjoy the path across. You are not living *your* dream. Dream careers are built by:

D Determination, not desperation
R Realization, not repetition
E Enthusiasm, not just experience
A Actualization, not just activity
M Mastery, not misery or mystery

In your dream career, you are in charge. You determine your future. You get an opportunity to realize your dreams. You work from enthusiasm, not just to get more experience. You are living your life, not just performing a set of activities. You are heading toward mastery of a skill, not just trying to avoid misery or doing something that you find a mystery because someone else is paying you to do it!

3. When should I go for my dream career and when should I get a transition J.O.B. as you call it?

That's a question for your gut—and your bank account. You're ready when you feel comfortable going for it. Most people need emotional and financial support in order to continue toward their dream career. This is something you'll have to determine.

Here's a scenario that might make things a little clearer, though: Ellen's dream career is to be a graphic designer. She's apprenticing at a small design agency two mornings a week and taking two courses a semester. But, since her classes and materials cost money and she's not getting paid for her apprenticeship, she needs a J.O.B.

She's working as a typesetter at a job that allows her some schedule flexibility for her classes and design work. It's clear that Ellen is taking positive steps toward her goal but she needs a little more experience before she can launch her dream career. Thus, it's entirely appropriate for her to have a J.O.B. to help get her there.

4. What if I'm not happy after making the change and the commitment to my dream career?

Many people are surprised to find out that even their dream career brings stress—both good and bad. I encourage people just to walk step by step through the first six weeks of the new career—it's a little like making a move—you have to tiptoe around the unpacked boxes until you are comfortable. The biggest question I get is, "How can I be happy living on less money." And here's what I say: Learn to cut costs, do without some of the luxuries you've become accustomed to, and get outside assistance if you absolutely need it. You might also consider subsidizing your income with a part-time J.O.B.

If you're truly unhappy, you may want to look at other factors—your social life, your personal life, your values, your spiritual fulfillment and what happiness means to you. Some clients determine that "making a significant contribution" with their lives means learning to deal with a certain amount of personal dissonance. But the payoffs often outweigh the waves of frustration.

5. I really want to have my own business but what if I regret it?

Starting your own business is one of the toughest things to do, according to some of my clients. You need capital, you need productive employees, you need luck, and maybe up to more than 100 hours of work a week if you want the business to support you. If you have another means of support, that is a different choice. Remember, many people who have their own businesses *do* have independent income, spousal income, family income, etc. Beware. Many times your business becomes your landlord or your employees be-come the reason you're working.

The best way to determine how you'll react when you have your own business is to work for a small business in your chosen field. Be sure to work long enough until you're sure you want to venture off on your own.

Sometimes if my clients are unsure, I say try a third option. Maybe you'd like to teach or have a partner or work on the staff of a management consulting or law firm that works with small businesses. Of course, many people start their businesses on the side and work full-time. The odds of that working depend on you, the type of business and many other factors.

6. I tried to have a dream career several years ago and it didn't work. What did I do wrong? I'm afraid to try again.

You may need a rest, you may need to be better prepared, you may need to have a better board of advisers and better transition skills. As Susan Jeffers says in her book, *Feel the Fear and Do It Anyway*, you *can* have your dream—thousands of other people are living theirs.

Take the time necessary to evaluate what went wrong with your plan. Maybe it was the right dream, but wrong time and place. An example used in this book referred to a woman who started a jewelry business that failed. Upon analysis, she discovered that she loved the experience of designing and making the jewelry. She just didn't like selling it. She gave it a second shot, this time involving a salesperson so she could concentrate on the part of the work she loved the most.

7. I think I'm failing, but I'm so busy I can't tell.

Stop! You may feel that you're too busy to jump off the treadmill, but it may be essential to your survival. Cut back your workload immediately, take a day off, drop your community work, get some counseling and assistance. If you run a business and you're in financial trouble, do what's necessary. Reduce your payroll if necessary—but take care of the situation. Don't use up all of your money. You need outside help to change your attitude and your bottom line. Get help today!

8. How long will it take me to reach my dream?

My average client makes a transition in 18 months, once he or she has established a goal, a path, and gets the dream on the road. For some, it takes three to seven years because they decide to go back to school. Others find it is a lifetime quest as they move from J.O.B. to transition career to dream career. Enjoy the trip—otherwise you won't enjoy the destination.

9. Do I have to go back to school to live out my dream career?

Possibly not, but you'll probably *never stop learning*. Continuing education is the only way to stay ahead. I know grade-school dropouts who live their dream and I have doctoral fellows who aren't even close to their quest. The difference is, the successful individuals are those who soak up new information—from any source they find.

It's a good idea to keep your eyes open for interesting and pertinent classes, workshops, seminars, conferences and lectures. Read up on your industry and related industries. Learn new skills that will enhance your work.

10. How do I get the money to start my business, pay for my schooling or allow me to make the transition?

My clients sell their cars, mortgage their houses, find investors or even get married to live out their dreams. I don't recommend that you take out large loans, but you may feel comfortable doing that. Ben and Jerry got investors throughout the state of Vermont to support the launch of their ice-cream company—you may find believers like those, too.

11. What do I do? I just declared bankruptcy. Can I dare to go for my dream career now?

If you're OK emotionally, you may be in a better position than you realize. You have no other financial obligations now (except the ones you morally feel you must pay back). Just remember, getting credit will be tough—not impossible, but tough.

Some of my clients have found that bankruptcy actually made them a better credit risk than when they were $80,000 in debt. You can get credit cards and even credit at some places, usually by making large cash deposits or by establishing personal relationships. You can even buy a car. And many people have been able to get landlords and homeowners to help them finance their dreams.

12. What are the best dream careers for the '90s and beyond?

In her book, *100 Best Jobs for the '90s and Beyond*, Carol Kleiman lists such standards as: financial planner, lawyer, management consultant, firefighter, psychologist, teacher, dentist, registered nurse, veterinarian, cook, actor, writer and interior designer.

Careers in high-tech, health care and service industries are anticipated to be the best bets for the coming millennium. But, I repeat, *your* dream career should come from your gut! Who cares if the most, best and highest-paying jobs are in nursing if you hate the sight of blood! It's important for you to have a sense of what's going on in the work force, but you should still pursue your dream.

I've found that the best dream careers are the ones that *you* create: a specialized travel agency for adventure tours, a guide service for historical sites in your area, a new product you invent: your own brand of apple/berry muffins that you sell to the local restaurants. Imagination should be your guide!

13. My dream career seems like an impossible dream! What are my chances of writing the great American novel/making a movie/becoming a movie star?

Your chances of writing a novel or making and starring in your own movie are better than ever before. But to guarantee it, you may have to *self-publish* the book or independently produce the film. Don't worry about how it'll get done—just start writing. You know my motto by now: If you have a dream, *you can do it*! Just start.

In the last three years, 18 of my clients have produced their own films and more than a dozen of these have been shown in theaters—the rest are available on video—*really*. Plus, I have a whole bookshelf of books by my clients.

Remember, many of my clients are people like you—experts in their fields who have suddenly found they had or wanted to take the time to pursue their dreams. Look at John Grisham's success with his books like *The Firm*. Don't be disappointed if fame doesn't come instantly. As William Saroyan has said, "It's not necessary for anything one writes to be instantly great, the important thing is for one to resign oneself to the truth that one is only a person, and to work..."

14. I'm a woman. What are my chances of owning my own business?

Experts say that by the year 2000, more than 50 percent of all businesses will be owned by women. Check out such organizations as the National Association of Women

Business Owners (NAWBO), and local women's referral services and networks for details and role models.

15. Can I work from my home? I'm raising a family.

Link Resources, a New York market research firm, predicts that within the next decade about one-third of all working people will work from home. We will be networked to offices—we will have modems and videophones to connect us not just with our companies but with "partners" around the world.

For the time being, however, there are still plenty of career opportunities that you can pursue from your home—especially if you have a computer with a word-processing program. Writing, editing, design, sales, catering, day care, tutoring, accounting—the list is as endless as your imagination.

16. How can I be sure that a robot won't be able to do my dream career better than I can?

Well, if you can build that kind of robot—you may have a very lucrative dream career! Seriously, even if you choose to go into such "futuristic" industries as biotechnology, genetics, telecommunications, high-tech entertainment, computers, lasers, medical technology and science and semiconductors, human psychology will still be the key ingredient; technology will be the tools. It's true that robots will be used in high-risk areas such as nuclear wastes, radioactive material disposal, etc. But in our lifetimes, robots will probably still work for *us*, not the other way around, according to the experts I've met.

17. Am I too old for my dream career?

The government estimate that 35.9 percent of the population will be over 45 by the year 2000 and 13 percent will be over 65. Americans over 50 consume more than $800 billion worth of goods and services. You'd do well if you're 60 or over to target your peers—consider dream career options in eldercare, tours for seniors, special foods for special diets, etc. You're never too old to live your dream!

18. What if I win the lottery? What should I do?

Surprisingly, statistics show that only 24 percent of state lottery workers stopped working within a year of hitting the jackpot. And that included 13 percent who were of retirement age when they won. Only 9 percent of those who won dropped out of the "rat race." Now, if you can find *those* people, they may have a yen to invest in your dream careers or dream businesses! Many of my clients say it's not the money that matters, it's the desire that sends them toward their dream careers and success.

19. How about me? I'm a minority—I'm black or Hispanic or Asian or...

You're in the driver's seat! If you plan it right you can move straight for your dream with SBA assistance, grants and more. Gordon Link, executive vice president at McCann Erickson Advertising in New York says, "the minority will become the majority." We'll live in a rainbow community of all races and ethnic backgrounds. I encourage my minority clients to use their racial background and ethnic heritage to cash in or create new trends in foods, clothing or other products and services.

20. I'm disabled. What about my future? How can I dare to dream about a career when I can't even get a job?

The impact of the Federal Americans with Disabilities Act of 1990 is just starting to be felt in the workplace. But the really good news is that in an information-driven society, your brainpower will be more important than your brawnpower. Plus, with a computer and modem, you can work conveniently from your home.

Check out local computer groups for details, or call your telephone company for information about their special adaptations for the disabled in the workplace. New computers that are voice-activated, like Apple's Plaintalk, underscore the potential for the disabled in workplace. Many local computer conferences such as the San Diego Computer Fair feature special programs for the disabled.

But don't be afraid to go for your real dream, too. There are troupes of disabled actors, blind painters, and even hearing-impaired cowboys riding the range in Montana. The movie "Waterdance" recounts the life story of Neal Jiminez (he also co-wrote the Bette Midler hit "For The Boys,"), who was severely disabled in an outdoor accident and now works from his wheelchair. It doesn't stop him from attending Hollywood premieres either.

21. Test your readiness

1. Are you ready for your dream career now? If so, why?

_____

_____

2. Why do you think you'd be happy doing/living your dream career? List three reasons:

_____

_____

_____

3. If you need to get a J.O.B., what are the reasons?

_____

_____

4. How can you begin to live out your dream career even if you're working at a J.O.B.? List four ways:

_____

_____

_____

_____

5. What payoffs does your dream career hold for you?

Security_____

Excitement_____

Personal freedom_____

Inner satisfaction_____

Other _____

_____

_____

_____

_____

What are the most compelling reasons for you to follow your dream? Complete these sentences:

As a child_____

_____

_____

I always knew_____

_____

_____

People told me (keep this positive)_____

_____

_____

A teacher once said_____

_____

_____

My spouse/partner believes_____

_____

_____

When I'm in my rocking chair, I want to have_____

_____

_____

The world will not be complete until I_____

_____

_____

In my dream career, I can make a difference because_____

_____

_____

I'm meant to follow my dream because_____

_____

_____

List your own reasons on a separate sheet. Be optimistic!

---

22. Beyond the dream: Building the bridge to the future

1. If you had to select three dream careers, what would they be?

_____

_____

_____

2. If money were no object, and you had no limitations, what would you do?

_____

_____

3. What career do you see yourself in in your 80s? If you hadn't thought about it, do so now and pick a career other than "retirement."

_____

_____

4. If you were 20 again, what career would you choose?

_____

_____

5. Why can't you follow that career now?

_____

_____

_____

6. How can you change things (yes, including the world) so that you could live out that dream?

_____

_____

_____

Your 18-Month Recareering Plan

A question I am asked frequently by clients and audience members is "How long will it take to change careers?"

As that query is spoken, voices crack with emotion, tears well up in the corners of the eyes of strong men and women.

For beneath the question "How long will it take?" surfaces a well filled with sheer terror for some and excitement and concern for others. When asking the "how long" question, people want to know much more. "Do you think I can do it?" "Do I have enough money to get through the transition?" "Have you ever met anyone who has made exactly this kind of career transition?"

Rather than give some vague answer, I have developed a proprietary strategy that shows you how you can make the career transition within 18 to 24 months from the time you have targeted your new career.

One client reminded me that 24 months is the gestation period for an elephant. Was that why I had chosen the figure I had? To many people, creating a new career is a little like giving birth to an elephant!

Actually, this period is based on my experience in launching hundreds of new products and services nationally as a packaged-goods marketing expert and former executive for ad agencies such as Foote, Cone & Belding. I have documented that on the average it takes a cycle of about 18 months to 2 years to see the product evolve from concept to fruition in the marketplace.

Because launching a new career is a lot like launching a new product, I've found that the same steps—somewhat modified—can be successfully applied to the recareering process.

My 18-Month Recareering Plan that I give to my clients is actually too involved and complex to present here in this book. It involves a lot of coaching, paperwork, exercises—and is also tailor-made for the individual. But I offer a solid skeletal structure that you can use to get started on the road to your new career.

If you're interested in knowing more about my 18-Month Recareering Plan, please write to me at Star*Course, 1714 Sanborn Ave., Los Angeles, CA 90027. I also encourage you to contact me for details about personal consultations, tapes, classes, corporate training seminars, motivational speeches—or just to give me any input on this book.

18-Month Recareering Plan

Months 1 to 3

Set the stage for success by clearly identifying your personal goals and lifestyle choices. (Any questions, reread Chapters 4 and 5 in this book.)

❑ 1. Clarify your career vision. (If you're not clear on what you want to do, spend the time necessary to get a better focus.)
❑ 2. Define your target profession (describe in detail).
❑ 3. Identify variations of this career. (If your goal is to be a writer, you might consider being a newspaper columnist, technical writer or novelist.)
❑ 4. Conduct a career audit. What experience and skills can you apply to your new career?
❑ 5. Make sure there's a good mesh between your career goals and your lifestyle goals. (If your target career is to be an ice-fishing guide and you want to live on a horse ranch in the desert, you may have some work to do.)
❑ 6. Evaluate your current financial status and develop a financial strategy. (Do you need a loan? Should you get a J.O.B?)
❑ 7. Identify any problems or threats to your career goals. Family objections? Financial limitations?

Notes: _____
_____
_____
_____
_____
_____

18-Month Recareering Plan

Months 3 to 6

Create your path and support system, using such tools as education, training and resource people.

❑ 1. Take care of unfinished business (divorce, legal problems, purchasing a home, marriage). Tie everything up so you can focus on recareering.

❑ 2. Research your target career (salary ranges, education requirements, apprenticeship opportunities, trends, etc.).

❑ 3. Enroll in any class you'll need before launching your career.

❑ 4. Learn to use a computer—*before* you buy!

❑ 5. Take the appropriate language course if you're planning to go into an international field or live abroad.

❑ 6. Select role models. Choose your role models to provide inspiration and advice.

❑ 7. Develop your list of industry contacts, expand your network.

Notes: _____

_____

_____

_____

_____

_____

_____

_____

_____

18-Month Recareering Plan

Months 6 to 9

Narrow the field and take care of day-to-day financial needs as you develop a clearer picture of how to approach your career plans. Begin to delve into your chosen field.

❑ 1. Identify several individuals in your career field. Learn as much as you can about them and from them (by inviting them for coffee, attending one of their seminars, reading their books, etc.).

❑ 2. Make a list of companies, employers or business opportunities you might target for the future when you're ready to start your dream career.

❑ 3. Create your personal board of advisers. Make sure all crucial areas—finance, marketing, sales, moral support—are covered.

❑ 4. Get a J.O.B. if necessary.

❑ 5. Or adapt your current job to help you have more time to prepare for something else—go to four days or change your hours so that you can go to classes or interviews or travel.

❑ 6. Attend conventions, seminars and workshops on your target career.

Notes: _____

_____

_____

_____

_____

_____

18-Month Recareering Plan

Months 9 to 12

Now is the time to begin building your expertise in your dream career.

☐ 1. Call a status meeting with your personal board of advisers.

☐ 2. Teach a workshop or seminar in your chosen field. Check out opportunities at work or at local community centers.

☐ 3. Create a series of 24-hour immersions or on-the-job experiences.

☐ 4. Get volunteer work in your new career field. (A great way to make contacts as well as gain experience.)

☐ 5. Be aware of your lifestyle, physical and emotional needs—and make sure you are getting nourished.

Notes: _____

_____

_____

_____

_____

_____

_____

_____

_____

_____

_____

_____

_____

18-Month Recareering Plan

Months 12 to 15

Develop something visible that reaches out and tells people you are living the dream.

☐ 1. Create a newsletter for your dream career or business. Mail to your list of networking contacts, potential employers or clients and other industry contacts.

☐ 2. Develop a book proposal about your chosen field.

☐ 3. Send out a press release or announcement about your career move or new business.

☐ 4. Develop a brochure for your new business. Work with a designer or writer with whom you may be able to trade services.

☐ 5. Get business cards and stationery.

Notes: _____

_____

_____

_____

_____

_____

_____

_____

_____

_____

_____

_____

_____

18-Month Recareering Plan

Months 15 to 18

Put the dream into action!

❑ 1. If you can't dive into it full-time just yet, do it part-time—or arrange to try it full-time on a temporary basis.

❑ 2. Set up a consulting practice in the field.

❑ 3. Celebrate your dream in progress—throw a party when you get the new job, open the boutique or sell your book.

❑ 4. Document your progress. Make a list of the top 20 accomplishments in the past year! Congratulate yourself!

Notes: _____

_____

_____

_____

_____

_____

_____

_____

_____

_____

_____

_____

_____

_____

18-Month Recareering Plan

Months 18 and beyond

It may take longer, so be prepared. This is the tough time when many give up. Depend on the following to help you through the difficult times:

❏ 1. Turn to your role models. Take a seminar, rent inspirational videos, read books, etc.

❏ 2. Expand your personal board of advisers. Turn to them for emotional and financial help if necessary.

❏ 3. *Work* your plan. Instead of worrying about how you're doing or if you're going to make it, just keep going for it.

❏ 4. Arrange to get some applause for your accomplishments. Speak at the Rotary Club or a Kiwanis meeting about your new career. Write an article for your alumni journal. Share your accomplishments with friends in a detailed letter.

❏ 5. Take a vacation. Get away and meet people who see you as only the new person with the new career. Brag about the good stuff—leave the challenges behind for a week or a weekend.

Notes: _____

_____

_____

_____

_____

_____

_____

_____

As I write this, it is June 21, the first day of summer. Being from the Midwest originally, where the change of seasons is very predominant, I still encourage my clients to use the first day of summer, fall, winter and spring as a touchstone to the future. On this day (or evening), they take stock of their progress and their path to the future. I encourage you to use the start of the four seasons as the dates to plan and schedule key steps for your career transition. But start today. Don't delay. And when the start of the new season comes around, *stop what you're doing and evaluate and determine whether you are on the right path or whether you have to adjust.*

One of the most valuable things I learned in visiting the Houston Space Center and going underground at NORAD (North American Aerial Defense Command) in Colorado Springs, was that most of the time the spacecraft is *off* course—it must constantly be put back on course. You'll find that making a career change may feel off-course to you—interference from family, money problems, crises in confidence and more will pull and tug you left and right. It's up to you to keep on track. Adjust or get additional help so you can reach your target—your dream career. Have a great trip.

For more information about successful recareering, please contact Joyce A. Schwarz at Star*Course. Here's a list of services available to you. Call for more details at 213-661-5225. Or write to Joyce at 1714 Sanborn Ave., Los Angeles, CA 90027.

- **Recareering and training consultation.** Corporate training and consultation available on such topics as "re-engineering your work force for the year 2000" and "redesigning your employee career paths." Daily, project and annual programs available. (Also customized programs and workshops for retirees, early retirees and downsizing efforts.)

- *Successful Recareering* **seminars.** Available for corporations and individuals. Call or write for brochure.

- *Successful Recareering* **18 month step-by-step workbook, audio tapes and video package.** Call or write for a promotional flyer.

- **Speeches and motivational talks.** On such topics as, "how to find your dream career." Available for your group or organization.

- **New millennium work styles.** Ten trends that will change you and your company forever.

Index

Successful Recareering